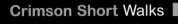

KT-496-235

North York Moors

Compiled and fully revised by
Dennis and Jan Kelsall

Acknowledgements
The authors wish to express their thanks to the staff of the North York Moors National Park and English Nature for their kind help.

Text:	Dennis and Jan Kelsall
Photography:	Dennis and Jan Kelsall
Editorial:	Ark Creative (UK) Ltd
Design:	Ark Creative (UK) Ltd

© Crimson Publishing, a division of Crimson Business Ltd

This product includes mapping data licensed from Ordnance Survey® with the permission of the Controller of Her Majesty's Stationery Office. © Crown Copyright 2009. All rights reserved. Licence number 150002047. Ordnance Survey, the OS symbol and Pathfinder are registered trademarks and Explorer, Landranger and Outdoor Leisure are trademarks of the Ordnance Survey, the national mapping agency of Great Britain.

ISBN 978-1-85458-519-6

While every care has been taken to ensure the accuracy of the route directions, the publishers cannot accept responsibility for errors or omissions, or for changes in details given. The countryside is not static: hedges and fences can be removed, field boundaries can be altered, footpaths can be rerouted and changes in ownership can result in the closure or diversion of some concessionary paths. Also, paths that are easy and pleasant for walking in fine conditions may become slippery, muddy and difficult in wet weather, while stepping stones across rivers and streams may become impassable.

If you find an inaccuracy in either the text or maps, please write to Crimson Publishing at the address below.

First published 2003
by Jarrold Publishing
Revised and reprinted 2006, 2009.

This edition first published in Great Britain 2009 by Crimson Publishing, a division of:
Crimson Business Ltd
Westminster House, Kew Road
Richmond, Surrey, TW9 2ND
www.totalwalking.co.uk

Printed in Singapore. 4/09

All rights reserved. No part of this publication may be reproduced, transmitted in any form or by any means, or stored in a retrieval system without either the prior written permission of the publisher, or in the case of reprographic reproduction a licence issued in accordance with the terms and licences issued by the CLA Ltd.

A catalogue record for this book is available from the British library.

Front cover: Bilsdale
Previous page: Sheep graze the lush lower slopes of Bilsdale

Contents

Keymap

SCALE 1:312 500 or 1 INCH to 5 MILES *1CM to 3.1 KM*

0   2   4   6   8   10 KILOMETRES   15

0   2   4   6   MILES   8   1

SPOT HEIGHTS SHOWN IN METRES

At-a-glance

Short walks up to 3½ miles

1	**2**	**3**	**4**
The Bridestones	*Kilburn White Horse*	*St Gregory's Minster*	*Falling Foss*
• Rock formations • Dalby Forest • nature trails • magnificent views	• White Horse • wonderful views • forest trails • good picnic spot	• Saxon church • 18th-century mill • woodland walk • unspoilt valley	• Waterfall • delightful woods • The Hermitage • nature trails
Walk Distance 1¾ miles (2.8km) **Time** 1 hour **Refreshments** Picnic tables by car park, refreshments at Low Dalby	**Walk Distance** 2 miles (3.2km) **Time** 1 hour **Refreshments** Picnic area by car park and Forresters' Arms in nearby Kilburn	**Walk Distance** 2½ miles (4km) **Time** 1 hour **Refreshments** None	**Walk Distance** 2½ miles (4km) **Time** 1½ hours **Refreshments** Falling Foss Tea Garden at Midge Hall
Clear paths throughout; moderate climb onto the moor	Steep climb on stepped path at start; woodland paths and tracks; *unguarded cliff edge*	Woodland and field paths with a short stretch along a quiet lane; short energetic climb	Woodland paths with undemanding ascents
p. 16	**p. 20**	**p. 24**	**p. 28**
Walk Completed ☐	Walk Completed ☐	Walk Completed ☐	Walk Completed ☐

5	6	7	8

Sutton Bank	*Danby Lodge to Clitherbeck*	*Rievaulx to Helmsley*	*Spout House and Bilsdale*
• Visitor Centre • stunning views • nature reserve • Gormire Lake	• The Moors Centre • open moorland • peaceful valley • picnic site	• Cistercian abbey • medieval castle • baroque mansion • Moorsbus service	• Old inn museum • enchanting views • green phone box • lovely Bilsdale
Walk Distance 2½ miles (4km) **Time** 1½ hours **Refreshments** Tearoom and picnic area at Visitor Centre	**Walk Distance** 3¼ miles (5.2km) **Time** 1½ hours **Refreshments** Tearoom and picnic area at Moors Centre	**Walk Distance** 3 miles (4.8km) **Time** 1½ hours **Refreshments** Choice of tearooms and pubs in Helmsley, tearoom at Rievaulx Abbey	**Walk Distance** 3½ miles (5.6km) **Time** 1½ hours **Refreshments** Drinks only are available from the Sun Inn
Woodland paths; *unguarded cliff edge;* prolonged ascent towards end	Moorland and field paths; moderate climbs	Clear tracks and paths with a short stretch along a country lane	Field paths and tracks; a short stretch on the road

p.32	p. 36	p. 40	p. 44
Walk Completed ☐	Walk Completed ☐	Walk Completed ☐	Walk Completed ☐

At-a-glance

Slightly longer walks of 3½ to 5 miles

9

Forge Valley and the River Derwent

10

Rosedale

11

Captain Cook's Monument

12

Nunnington

• Deep ravine	• Tranquil valleys	• Breathtaking views	• Water mill
• woodland walks	• attractive village	• picnic site	• country house
• nature reserve	• splendid views	• monument	• medieval church
• disabled access	• former priory site	• Captain Cook	• riverside walk

Walk Distance
3¾ miles (6km)
Time
2 hours
Refreshments
Pub at East Ayton 1½ miles (2.4km), picnic area beside car park

Walk Distance
4 miles (6.4km)
Time
2 hours
Refreshments
Choice of pubs and cafés in the village

Walk Distance
4 miles (6.4km)
Time
2 hours
Refreshments
Choice of pubs and cafés in Great Ayton 2 miles (3.2km)

Walk Distance
4¼ miles (6.8km)
Time
2 hours
Refreshments
Tearoom at Nunnington Hall and the Royal Oak in Nunnington village

---

Initial steep climb; *narrow path across steep slope.* Also, 'easy going' riverside trail suitable for prams and wheelchairs

Field and woodland paths; moderate climbs

Woodland paths and tracks; *very steep climb through Ayton Banks Wood*

Field tracks and paths, moderate climb

p. 48
Walk Completed ☐

p. 52
Walk Completed ☐

p. 57
Walk Completed ☐

p. 61
Walk Completed ☐

13	**14**	**15**	**16**

Staithes	*Robin Hood's Bay*	*Hutton-le-Hole and Lastingham*	*Byland Abbey*
• Delightful village • dramatic cliff walk • heritage centre • nature reserve	• Fossil beach • heritage museum • cliff walk • coastal views	• Folk museum • 11th-century crypt • pretty villages • moorland views	• Woodland • country pub • Cistercian abbey • countryside views
Walk Distance 4½ miles (7.2km) **Time** 2 hours **Refreshments** Choice of pubs in Staithes and Fox and Hounds at Dalehouse	**Walk Distance** 4¾ miles (7.6km) **Time** 2¼ hours **Refreshments** Choice of pubs and cafés in Robin Hood's Bay	**Walk Distance** 5 miles (8km) **Time** 2½ hours **Refreshments** Inn and teashops at Hutton-le-Hole and Blacksmiths Arms in Lastingham	**Walk Distance** 5 miles (8km) **Time** 2½ hours **Refreshments** Wombwell Arms at Wass
Field and woodland paths; *sustained climb; exposed cliffs*	Coast path and disused railway line; unfenced cliffs; moderate climb	Field paths and tracks, with short section on lane; *steep climb*	Field and woodland paths with sustained ascents
p.65	**p. 70**	**p. 74**	**p. 78**
Walk Completed ☐	Walk Completed ☐	Walk Completed ☐	Walk Completed ☐

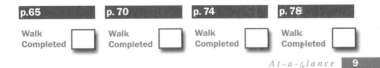

At-a-glance

17

Hole of Horcum

18

Mallyan Spout

19

Ravenscar

20

Farndale

• Steam railway • dramatic views • smugglers' inn • stunning moors	• Waterfall • steam railway • attractive village • *Heartbeat* country	• Old alum works • Coastal Centre • splendid moors • coastal views	• Stunning views • pretty hamlets • evocative moors • unspoilt valleys
Walk Distance 5¼ miles (8.4km)	**Walk Distance** 5¼ miles (8.4km)	**Walk Distance** 6½ miles (10.5km)	**Walk Distance** 6½ miles (10.5km)
Time 2½ hours	**Time** 2½ hours	**Time** 3 hours	**Time** 3 hours
Refreshments None	**Refreshments** Choice of pubs and tearooms at Goathland. Pub at Beck Hole	**Refreshments** Bar snacks and meals at Raven Hall Hotel, drinks at Coastal Centre	**Refreshments** Seasonal café at High Mill and pub near route at Church Houses

---

Moorland paths and steep climbs; *unguarded cliff edge*	Moor and woodland paths; moderate climbs	Moorland tracks and disused railway line; moderate climbs	Field paths and moorland tracks, sustained but moderate climb

---

p. 83	p. 88	p. 93	p. 98
Walk Completed ☐	Walk Completed ☐	Walk Completed ☐	Walk Completed ☐

Introduction

The North York Moors are deservedly recognised as one of the most beautiful regions of England, but 'moor' is hardly sufficient to describe the diversity of landscapes and multiplicity of appeal that exist within its bounds. Seen in the vague half-light of a wet and windy winter's afternoon, the earlier name of Blackamore – 'black hill moor' - is perhaps a fitting description for the awesome vastness of its rolling upland, where hardly anything, be it the work of nature or man, interrupts the long skyline. Yet witness it again, illuminated by a shaft of sunlight stabbing through low, scudding clouds, or clad in regal splendour by the flowering ling, and you will realise that it is a place of endless change, where each passing hour brings a subtle variation of mood.

Dales, woods and sea

Wander into its secluded dales and you will discover a different world, where sparkling streams cascade over rocky beds and tree-fringed rivers snake across lush grass meadows. Idyllic villages and picturesque farmsteads nestle within their folds, surrounded by orderly fields that probe the limits of viable cultivation. In some places the land is silvan, but not all is commercial forest, for there remain many places where native species prevail, harking back to the wild woodland that once covered much of the country. And, in the east, rugged cliffs, sheltered coves and sweeping sands draw an erratic boundary between the opposing elements of land and sea. Everywhere has its own character and charm, and invites a leisurely exploration and contemplation.

Human enterprise

Yet this wild and beautiful landscape is not necessarily all that it appears, for the hand of man has played a far greater role in shaping the countryside than you might at first think. Throughout, the high moors bear evidence of prehistoric settlement, in scattered burial mounds, territorial boundary dykes and agricultural enclosures; traces of the first farmers who tamed the primeval uplands. Early medieval monks also left their mark, not only in the evocative ruins of the vast monastic houses raised in isolated valleys, but by managing the uplands as immense sheep walks. They organised mining for iron and coal, enterprises, which, during the Industrial Revolution, turned some of the remotest settlements into boom towns almost overnight. Quarrying for stone, alum and other minerals changed the face of the moors and a considerable network of tramways and railways rapidly reached out to service them. The coast, too, was alive with activity; the few safe landings along its rocky and dangerous shores were among the most productive fishing villages on the whole of the English eastern seaboard, and Whitby grew to be both a major trading port and whaling station. For better or worse, those days and their industry have long passed, and a new balance between man's activities and nature prevails. The legacy is a land still rich in natural beauty, enhanced by the relics left behind by the trail of human toil and endeavour.

A place to walk

Sparsely populated and with relatively few roads, the Moors are best explored on foot, and there are some 1,400 miles of designated rights of way as well as many other paths and tracks along which it is permissible to walk. Some of these date from the monastic era and were, in effect, the motorways of their day, connecting the monasteries with their outlying granges and the markets to which produce was taken. As you roam across the open moors, you will come across stone-flagged paths and isolated standing stones, crosses

Looking towards the head of West Gill

and markers, set up in antiquity to guide travellers safely across this otherwise featureless expanse. One of the best-known is Young Ralph's Cross at the head of Rosedale, which has been adopted as the emblem of the North York Moors National Park. It encompasses some 544 square miles (1,436 km²) and is the third most visited of the country's National Parks.

Discover the countryside
With so many pathways and different places to visit, the difficulty is not in finding somewhere to go, but rather deciding just where to begin. A good place, particularly if you are new to the area, is one of the two National Park centres, which are located at Danby and Sutton Bank. Fascinating displays and exhibitions offer an ideal introduction, and the short walks from each illustrate disparate aspects of the moor, demonstrating its capacity for beauty and surprise. Other walks in this collection reveal some of the Moor's most outstanding natural features; the dramatic Hole of Horcum,

the enigmatic rocks at Bridestones and the splendid tumbling waters of Falling Foss. As well as exploring the high moors, where the strange calling of the grouse is never far away, wander through verdant dales such as the beautiful Farndale, whose Lenten lilies carpet the riverside meadows in celebration of spring's arrival. In contrast are areas that were exploited by industry, such as the coastal cliffs at Ravenscar, excavated for their alum-bearing shale, or the now peaceful village and valley of Rosedale, once filled with 'work hard, play hard' miners who dug into the hillside for its rich iron ore.

Other places to visit
Follow these walks to discover some fascinating ancient buildings; the atmospheric ruins of the great abbey communities at Rievaulx and Byland or the stark, defensive, medieval stone pile at Helmsley. Very different is the magnificently restored Duncombe Park and, at Nunnington, there is another splendid country house to visit. The small market towns and picturesque villages, from which many of the routes begin also have much of interest and are worthy of exploration, particularly their churches, often the oldest building standing. Other walks pass fine museums, while at Spout House you will find a wonderfully preserved country inn, and if you fancy a ride on a steam train, there is even one ramble that utilises the North York Moors Railway. Above all, this collection of walks is about enjoyment, and in each one, short or long, you will find that there is much to delight.

Choosing a walk
The routes and information in this book have been devised specifically with families and children in mind. The purpose is not simply to get between two points but to enjoy discovering the many aspects of the countryside. All the walks include points of interest and perhaps a suggestion for somewhere to visit along the way as well as questions to encourage enquiring young minds.

The walks are graded by length and difficulty and if you, or your children have not walked before, choose from the shorter walks for your first outings. But note that the Moors landscape is far from flat and even the shorter routes involve brief climbs. Many of the walks lend themselves to variation and consideration of the map will often suggest a shorter or longer ramble. Remember that the countryside is a living and working entity and is constantly changing. Landmarks can disappear, stiles may be replaced by gates and even rights of way are occasionally altered. However, attention to the route descriptions, reference to the maps and a little common sense will get you around without trouble. An indication of what to expect along the way is given under the Route Features for each walk, but the precise nature of the ground underfoot will depend upon the season and recent weather conditions; paths can be muddy at any time of the year and luxuriant summer vegetation means that shorts are not always a good idea. If you do set out on a walk and discover that the going is harder than you expected, or the weather has deteriorated, do not be afraid to turn back. The route will always be there for another day, when you are fitter, the children are more experienced or the weather is kinder.

This book includes a list of waypoints alongside the description of the walk, so that you can enjoy the full benefits of gps should you wish to.

For more information on using your gps, read the *Pathfinder® Guide GPS for Walkers*, by gps teacher and navigation trainer, Clive Thomas (ISBN 978-0-7117-4445-5).

For essential information on map reading and basic navigation, read the *Pathfinder® Guide Map Reading Skills* by outdoor writer, Terry Marsh (ISBN 978-0-7117-4978-8). Both titles are available in bookshops or can be ordered online at www.totalwalking.co.uk

The Bridestones

■ **Rock formations**   ■ **nature trails**
■ **Dalby Forest**   ■ **magnificent views**

walk 1

Although many pathways and tracks penetrate Dalby Forest, this short circuit is as spectacular as any you might choose. It leads through a delightful valley before rising onto the moor above, where wind, rain and frost have carved the curious outcropping rocks of the Bridestones into weird and wonderful shapes.

On top of High Bridestones

walk 1

START Low Staindale off Dalby Forest Drive (toll road)

DISTANCE 1¾ miles (2.8km)

TIME 1 hour

PARKING Car park at start of walk

ROUTE FEATURES Clear paths throughout; moderate climb onto the moor

GPS WAYPOINTS
SE 877 905
Ⓐ SE 872 905
Ⓑ SE 872 914
Ⓒ SE 873 909

PUBLIC TRANSPORT Sunday, Bank Holiday and daily summer Moorsbus service to Low Staindale 3 miles (4.8km)

REFRESHMENTS Picnic tables by car park, refreshments at Low Dalby Visitor Centre 3 miles (4.8km)

PUBLIC TOILETS Above car park

PLAY AREA By Visitor Centre

ORDNANCE SURVEY MAPS Explorer OL27 (North York Moors – Eastern area)

A path leads west from the back of the car park across an open meadow towards trees. As it then swings right, leave through a kissing-gate and continue along the valley below the edge of a wood. Approaching a stream, look for a sign directing you right to the Bridestones Ⓐ.

Pass through a kissing-gate into Dove Dale. Over a bridge, continue by the beck, later re-crossing higher up at the mouth of Bridestones Griff. Climb a well-made path that gains height along the ridge separating the two valleys, pausing to look out across

> The two groups of strangely weathered rocks that break the emptiness of the open moor are known as **High and Low Bridestones** respectively. They are composed of stone, which was laid down during the Jurassic period some 150 million years ago. Differential erosion of the layers by the action of frost, wind and rain has, because of their varying hardness, produced the bizarre shapes we see today.

the valley where some of the Bridestones come into view on the skyline. Levelling at the top, the way continues easily over heather heath, leading you to the first of the fantastic formations. Where the track then splits Ⓑ, go right.

The Pepper Pot

Walking into Dove Dale

The derivation of the name **'Bridestones'** is not certain, but is perhaps a corruption of 'Brinkstones' from the Norse language and refers to their position above the rim of the valley. An alternative theory, however, suggests that the rocks may have been the focus of an ancient fertility ceremony. And, of course, there is always a more romantic explanation; one story tells that a young couple, crossing the moor after their wedding, were suddenly engulfed in mist and sought temporary refuge among the rocks until it cleared.

Dip across the head of the valley, crossing a stream and rising to a fork. Go right to follow the rim of the valley, passing the rocks seen earlier as you climbed onto the ridge. As you pass the last of the formations 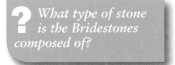**C**, ignore a path off left and continue ahead, the way gradually giving up height towards a clump of birch trees.

Beyond, the path turns to fall more steeply, dropping through woodland back into Stain Dale. At the bottom of the hill, go right

> **?** *What type of stone is the Bridestones composed of?*

as a path joins from the left and then swing left by the kissing-gate to retrace your steps to the car park. ∎

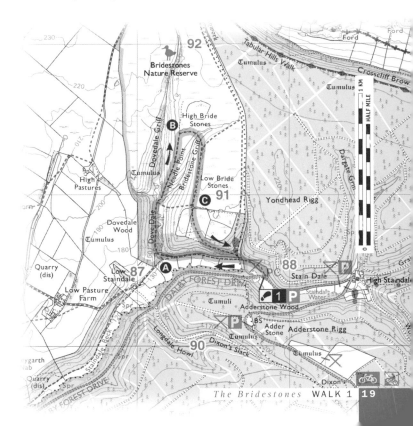

Kilburn White Horse

■ **White Horse**   ■ **forest trails**
■ **wonderful views**   ■ **good picnic spot**

walk 2

The best views of the White Horse are to be had from a mile or so away to the south west, but it is an impressive sight even at close range. From the top of the cliff the prospect towards the Vale of York is spectacular and there is often the added treat of gliders soaring into the sky from the flying club just behind.

The Kilburn White Horse is a local landmark

walk **2**

START White Horse, near Kilburn

DISTANCE 2 miles (3.2km)

TIME 1 hour

PARKING Car park at start of walk

ROUTE FEATURES Steep climb on stepped path at start; woodland paths and tracks; *unguarded cliff edge*

GPS WAYPOINTS

SE 514 812
Ⓐ SE 515 818
Ⓑ SE 512 817
Ⓒ SE 507 813

PUBLIC TRANSPORT Sunday, Bank Holiday and daily summer Moorsbus service to Kilburn and Sutton Bank 1½ miles (2.4km)

REFRESHMENTS Picnic area by car park and Forresters' Arms in nearby Kilburn 1½ miles (2.4km)

PUBLIC TOILETS Nearest at Sutton Bank Visitor Centre 1½ miles (2.4km)

PLAY AREA None

ORDNANCE SURVEY MAPS Explorer OL26 (North York Moors – Western area)

Inspired by Thomas Taylor and cut by volunteers headed by the village schoolmaster, the turf figure at Kilburn is the only **white horse** in the north of England. Some 314 feet (96m) long and nearly 228 feet (69m) high, it is said that two-dozen people can sit on the grass left undisturbed for its eye. As the underlying rock is an unremarkable dull brown, limewash was applied to make it stand out. Today, however, the villagers spread chalk chippings instead when giving it a periodic spring clean.

From the car park a steep flight of steps climbs beside the White Horse to the top of the scarp. To the left, a good path then follows the cliff edge around the perimeter of the airfield. After ¾ mile (1.2km), at a red-topped marker post Ⓐ, go left onto a narrower path that doubles back in an oblique descent. On the way down, openings in the trees allow more splendid vistas across the plain and to the cliffs of Sutton Bank farther north. As the gradient eases at the bottom of the hill, watch for a path joining from the right Ⓑ.

To the left, it undulates through the trees at the base of the cliff for ½ mile (800m) and offers a quick return to the car park. The main route, however, lies to the right, but almost immediately, leave sharp left along a marked bridleway that drops into the lower

A forester at work in the Hood Hill Plantation

? In what year was the White Horse cut?

forest. Keep ahead when you later cross a green track, carrying on down to emerge onto a foresters' road **C**.

Walk briefly left to a green-topped marker post and there make an acute left turn onto a wide, rising path. After a sharp, right-hand bend, the ascent continues, soon joining a higher track. With most of the climbing now behind you, follow it right and then, when you arrive at a fork, bear left. Reaching the next junction, go left and then right, rising to a broader path. The car park lies a short distance to the right.

✳ Born in 1876 in nearby **Kilburn**, Robert Thompson was the son of a carpenter and wheelwright. He developed a talent for woodcarving and soon achieved a reputation for producing fine oak furniture and ecclesiastical fittings. His trademark was a tiny carved mouse, which the craftsman worked into the decoration of every piece he made. Many of the local churches contain examples of Thompson's work, but his fame spread far beyond his native Yorkshire and you will even find the Mouseman's mark in Westminster Abbey. He died in 1955, but the workshop he founded continues in the village and his cottage is a showroom for its beautiful products.

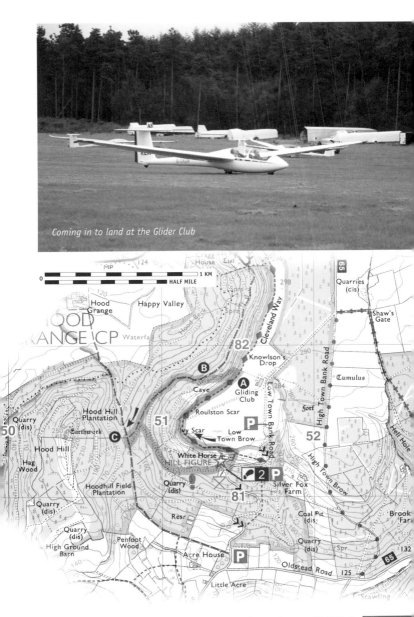

Coming in to land at the Glider Club

St Gregory's Minster

- Saxon church
- 18th-century mill
- woodland walk
- unspoilt valley

Secluded in woodland at the foot of a steep gorge, the ancient church of St Gregory's Minster has a fascinating history. The unspoilt valley behind winds for miles into the very heart of the moors, but you do not have to wander far to discover its serene beauty.

walk 3

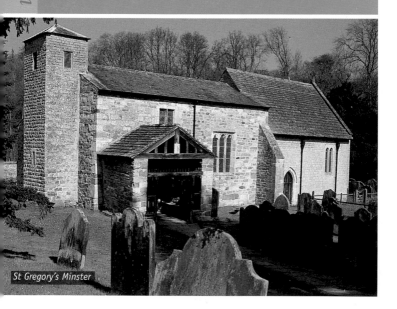

St Gregory's Minster

walk **3**

START St Gregory's Minster, Kirkdale

DISTANCE 2½ miles (4km)

TIME 1 hour

PARKING Park in the overflow car park (not in front of the church on Sundays)

ROUTE FEATURES Woodland and field paths with a short stretch along a quiet lane; short energetic climb *Note: The bridge across Hodge Beck behind the church (SE 675 859) has been washed away and, occasionally, after exceptionally heavy rain, the crossing is impassable. If in doubt, have a look before beginning the walk.*

GPS WAYPOINTS

 SE 676 856
Ⓐ SE 670 862
Ⓑ SE 668 869
Ⓒ SE 674 869

PUBLIC TRANSPORT Bus services to Kirkby Moorside 1½ mile (2.4km)

REFRESHMENTS None

PUBLIC TOILETS None

PLAY AREA None

ORDNANCE SURVEY MAPS Explorer OL26 (North York Moors – Western area)

Go back to the junction at the head of the lane leading to the church, where a waymark indicates a bridlepath up the wooded banking on the right. Emerging into a field at the top, swing right above Kirkdale Wood West. Part-way along the second field, cross into the trees before shortly emerging onto a lane Ⓐ.

Turn right and follow the lane down through the wood, passing a ruined lime kiln half-hidden in the trees on your left. Eventually arriving at Hold Caldron, walk on past the front of the old mill to cross a stone bridge spanning Hodge Beck Ⓑ.

Just over the bridge, turn through a gate on the right onto a woodland track, which rises steadily through the trees. At a fork,

★ The term 'minster' equates to 'mission', and it is possible that the first chapel here was an outpost associated with the 7th-century monastery at Lastingham. There was certainly a church on the spot in about 750, and two elaborately carved tombstones from its early period still lie inside the church. Perhaps the most remarkable relic, however, is an inscribed **Saxon sundial**, built into the south wall above the doorway. Inscribed in Old English, it commemorates the rebuilding of the church by Orm, son of Gamel in the days of King Edward and Earl Tostig, around 1060.

bear left and continue climbing, passing a second fork to reach a junction at the top. Go left and keep ahead to a gate out of the trees just above. Walk directly away across the field beyond.

? *What purpose did the steps that stand beside the lane near the church serve?*

In the fields above Cat Scar

At the far side **C**, follow the perimeter right to a gate, from which a path drops to a track at the head of Kirkdale Howl.

Turn sharp right and walk into a deepening wooded valley, keeping left at successive forks. At a three-fingered bridleway sign at the bottom, go left above the stream bed.

* In a **cave,** discovered near the church in 1821, quarrymen found hundreds of bones and teeth. Examination showed them to be the remains of elephants, bears, tigers and other animals, thought to have been killed by hyenas some 70,000 years ago.

Take the right branch at the next fork to emerge from the trees into a meadow. Keep ahead, crossing the usually dry bed of the river to return to St Gregory's Minster. ▪

*For much of the year, the riverbed by the church is quite dry, yet, beneath the bridge at **Hold Caldron** is an ample flow that once powered the corn mill there. The valley runs through limestone and the waters disappear below ground soon after the bridge, travelling through a subterranean channel to emerge downstream.

The woodland floors are splashed with yellow primroses in spring

Falling Foss

- **Waterfall**
- **delightful woodland**
- **The Hermitage**
- **nature trails**

walk 4

Approaching the end of their 178-mile (300km) trek, 'Coast to Coast' walkers often tarry in Littlebeck's enchanting, ravine-like valley before bracing muscle and sinew for the final stage to the North Sea. This pretty woodland ramble past a splendid waterfall, Falling Foss, and a curious rock shelter known as The Hermitage, gives a taste of the many sights encountered along the way.

The Hermitage

walk 4

START May Beck, end of minor lane 1¾ miles (2.8km) south of B1416

DISTANCE 2½ miles (4km)

TIME 1½ hours

PARKING Car park at start of walk

ROUTE FEATURES Woodland paths with undemanding ascents

GPS WAYPOINTS
⬛ NZ 892 024
Ⓐ NZ 888 034
Ⓑ NZ 885 040
Ⓒ NZ 885 037
Ⓓ NZ 888 033

PUBLIC TRANSPORT None available

REFRESHMENTS Falling Foss Tea Garden at Midge Hall

PUBLIC TOILETS None

PLAY AREA None

ORDNANCE SURVEY MAPS Explorer OL27 (North York Moors – Eastern area)

From the car park, cross the bridge and immediately turn downstream along a signed footpath to Falling Foss. Taking a higher line, it later passes through a gate into thicker woodland and subsequently crosses a side stream. At a fork just beyond, bear left, returning to May Beck at a ford. You can cross there or carry on a little farther above the eastern bank to a stone bridge Ⓐ.

Continuing north, re-cross the stream over a wooden footbridge to pass in front of Midge Hall. Forking left beyond, there is then a grand view of Falling Foss. Stick with the main path above the near precipitous wooded gorge to a junction and go left again, the way now signed to Littlebeck.

Cut from solid sandstone and entered by an impressive Gothic doorway, **The Hermitage's** roomy circular chamber, around which runs a surprisingly comfortable (at least after a long day's walking) stone bench, provides an ideal lunchtime shelter on a rainy day. Perched above it are a couple of 'chairs' fashioned from boulders. Sit in one and make a wish then sit in the other for it to come true or so the local story goes. But be careful clambering up, if you slip, you will be wishing that you had instead simply sat on the belvedere in front of the shelter to enjoy the view. The initials above the entrance are of George Chubb, who was schoolmaster in the nearby village of Littlebeck.

Falling Foss

After heavy rain, **Falling Foss** is a tremendous spectacle as May Beck plunges over a 50-foot (15-m) ledge in a torrent of spray and white foam. The nearby cottage, **Midge Hall**, was built by Sir James Wilson for his gamekeeper, but at the beginning of the 20th century was opened by Mrs Robinson as a tearoom. After years of dereliction and a brief spell as a museum, it has been restored and once again offers tasty home-cooked hospitality to walkers passing through this stunningly beautiful valley.

The undemanding path wanders on through the trees passing a second junction to reach The Hermitage **B**.

Turn around as if to retrace your steps, but immediately bear right on an oblique path that descends to the stream far below **C**. Cross the bridge over May Beck but ignore a second bridge just beyond and instead follow a path climbing from the valley. As it crests, the path swings right, falling to cross a side brook. The path then winds on to meet a gravel track **D**.

There is now another chance to visit the Falling Foss Tea Garden at Midge Hall, which lies just to the left. The way back, however, is to the right. Abandon the track almost immediately in favour of a path on the left that meanders away through the wood. Ignore stiles passed later on the right, eventually reaching a third stile beside a bridle gate. Go through the gate and follow the descending path back to the car park.

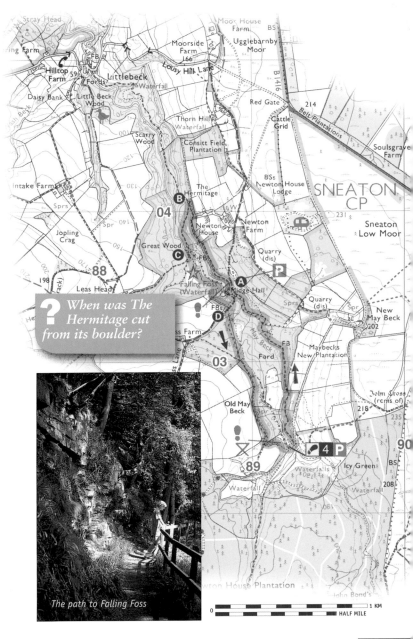

When was The
Hermitage cut
from its boulder?

The path to Falling Foss

Sutton Bank

walk 5

- Visitor Centre
- stunning views
- nature reserve
- Gormire Lake

For many visitors, the sharply twisting, steep road negotiating Sutton Bank is the gateway to the North York Moors National Park. From the top, there is a magnificent view to Yorkshire's other National Park, the Dales. After following the cliff edge, this walk drops through attractive woodland to Gormire Lake, unusual in that no streams either feed or drain it.

The view from Sutton Brow

walk 5

START Sutton Bank National Park Visitor Centre

DISTANCE 2½ miles (4km)

TIME 1½ hours

PARKING Car park at Visitor Centre (Pay and Display)

ROUTE FEATURES Woodland paths; *unguarded cliff edge;* prolonged ascent towards end

GPS WAYPOINTS
- SE 516 830
- Ⓐ SE 508 840
- Ⓑ SE 502 837
- Ⓒ SE 503 832

PUBLIC TRANSPORT Bus services to Sutton Bank

REFRESHMENTS Tearoom and picnic area at Visitor Centre

PUBLIC TOILETS Beside Visitor Centre

PLAY AREA None

ORDNANCE SURVEY MAPS Explorer OL26 (North York Moors – Western area)

White Mare Crag

William Wordsworth climbed **Sutton Bank** with his sister, Dorothy, in July 1802, during a journey to Brompton where his soon-to-be wife, Mary Hutchinson, lived. The breathtaking vista inspired the poet to write a sonnet, while Dorothy remarked in her journal on the cattle that were being herded from Scotland along the Hambleton Hills drove to be sold in the market at York.

Cross the picnic area and car park behind the Visitor Centre to the junction of a lane with the main road at the top of Sutton Bank. Cross the lane to a footpath opposite, signed 'Cleveland Way' and 'Sneck Yate', which follows the top of Sutton Brow. Initially in woodland, the way later emerges onto more open heath, giving some splendid views across the Vale of Mowbray.

After ¾ mile (1.2km) the path loses height easily before turning right around the overgrown corner of the wall.

A little farther on, leave the Cleveland Way, going sharp left onto a descending bridleway, signed 'Thirlby Bank' **A**. After first falling across shrubby heath, the route soon drops into woodland, winding steeply down through the trees along the course of an old banked way. Ignore side paths until, eventually you reach a junction at the bottom of the hill by a three-fingered bridleway sign **B**.

At the top of the path from Gormire Lake

Turn left and almost immediately, fork right along a gently undulating track towards Gormire Lake. Keep left with the main path where it later splits again, soon arriving at the lake shore, which, on a fine day, makes a grand spot for a picnic. At a signpost, a little farther on **C**, turn from the water's edge to climb through the trees on a path signed to the National Park Centre.

Many fantastic stories are told about **Gormire,** several featuring a white horse, which accounts, in part, for the figure cut into the scar above Kilburn. One legend attributes the lake's creation to the Devil who, astride a galloping mount, plunged to earth off the cliff leaving behind a bottomless crater. A sadder tale describes the tragedy of a young maid, whose white mare slipped, carrying her over the cliff to her death in the lake.

(If you reach a junction and sign to the A170 by a gate into Gormire Farm, you have gone some 200 yds (183m) too far.) Over a stile part-way up, keep on through the Garbutt Wood Nature Reserve to a fork. Go right, shortly passing a large isolated boulder at the edge of a clearing. Beyond, the gradient, having briefly eased, resumes its upward trend and there is a final stiff pull to the top of Sutton Bank. Here, you rejoin the Cleveland Way. Turn right and follow it back to the Visitor Centre. ■

> **?** *Look hard at the 'National Park tree' sculpture in the Visitor Centre foyer. What can you find worked into its branches?*

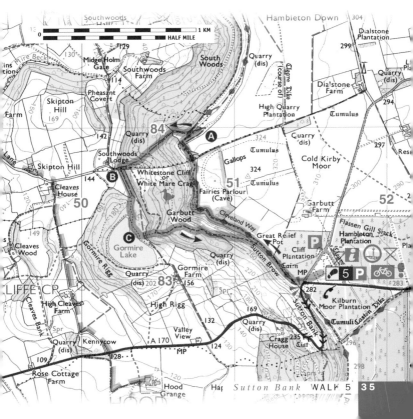

Danby Lodge to Clitherbeck

- The Moors Centre
- open moorland
- peaceful valley
- picnic site

If you have not visited the North York Moors before, the Moors Centre is an ideal place to begin your exploration, where exhibitions explain the area's history and its influence on the countryside we enjoy today. Discover on this route something of the vast emptiness of the open moor and the seclusion of its sheltered valleys, two contrasting features of a wonderful landscape.

walk 6

Lord's Turnpike

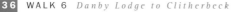

walk **6**

START Danby Lodge Moors Centre

DISTANCE 3¼ miles (5.2km)

TIME 1½ hours

PARKING Car park opposite Danby Lodge (Pay and Display)

ROUTE FEATURES Moorland and field paths; moderate climbs

GPS WAYPOINTS

 NZ 717 083
Ⓐ NZ 712 090
Ⓑ NZ 711 100
Ⓒ NZ 716 099

PUBLIC TRANSPORT Rail service to Danby 1 mile (1.6km), Sunday, Bank Holiday and daily summer Moorsbus service to Danby Lodge

REFRESHMENTS Tearoom and picnic area at Moors Centre

PUBLIC TOILETS At Moors Centre

PLAY AREA None

ORDNANCE SURVEY MAPS Ordnance survey map Explorer OL27 (North York Moors – Eastern area)

Leaving the car park, turn right past the Moors Centre to a junction. Opposite, a waymarked track rises through a wood. Continue above open ground for another 150 yds (137m) and turn through the second gate on the left. Head upfield, in a little while forking right. Ignore a crossing grass track and carry on parallel with the right-hand wall. Bend with it higher up as tracks join from the left, staying with the wall just a short distance to reach a gate Ⓐ.

There, go left along a prominent undulating path across the immense openness of the moor. Some 300 years ago this lonely upland was mined for its coal, which lies in shallow seams just below the surface. You can still see evidence of the activity in the heather-covered hollows and mounds that lie beside the path. Stroll on for almost ¾ mile (1.2km) to meet a road Ⓑ.

The moors around **Danby** were not always desolate and featureless and there is ample evidence to show that 3,000 years ago, during the Bronze Age, it supported a relatively large population. Numerous barrows, field enclosures and settlement sites have been identified on the riggs above the deep valleys, as well as a 5-foot (2m) high monolith, once part of a 42-foot (13m) diameter stone circle.

The stile beside Clitherbeck Farm

Walk right, crossing Black Beck, but then a few paces after it, turn off right to a gate set back from the road. Follow the field edge away, continuing across the enclosure beyond to Clitherbeck Farm. Leave the yard straight away along a track on the left, which in due course leads to a junction. To the right, the way descends gently to a bend and crosses Clither Beck. Almost immediately mount a stile on the right, follow the stream down for some 250 yds (239m) then, by a sycamore tree, leave the path left and briefly climb beside a wall to a gate on the right **C**.

An old track passes the ruin of a tiny farmstead, ending through another gate. Back on the edge of the open moor, keep ahead, initially guided by a wall. Curve right beyond its end, now on a clear path that falls gently along the side of a very pretty valley. Over a ladder stile at the bottom, continue beside a stream to a footbridge. On the opposite bank, go left to a gate and on across bracken meadow below a bank planted with saplings. More gates take the way ahead, rising through the young plantation before climbing across rough pasture to join a wall at the top. Walk left, now retracing your outward steps back to Danby Lodge. ■

✱ Originally a simple farmhouse overlooking the River Esk, **Danby Lodge** was extended in the 19th century into a comfortable shooting lodge. It has been the National Park Information Centre since 1976.

? *Across a stream behind the car park there is a delightful wood to explore, what bird is it named after?*

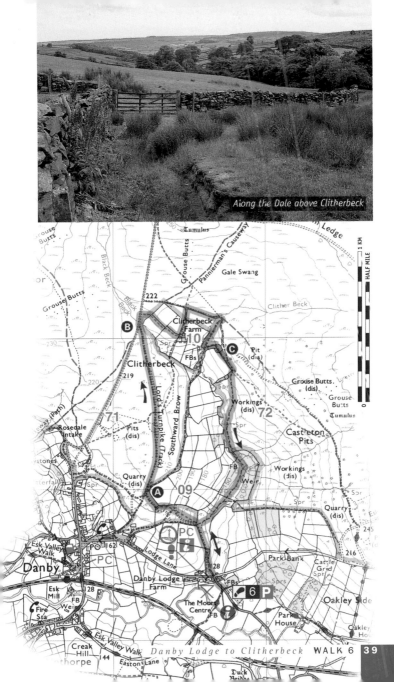

Along the Dale above Clitherbeck

Rievaulx to Helmsley

- ■ Cistercian abbey (EH)
- ■ medieval castle (EH)
- ■ baroque mansion
- ■ Moorsbus service

There is much to see at both ends of this one-way walk, which takes advantage of the seasonal Moorsbus service, that leaves the market place in Helmsley by the monument. Parking is very limited at Rievaulx, and on days when the Moorsbus service does not operate, the distance is not so great as to preclude following it there and back from the attractive ancient market town.

walk 7

Rievaulx Abbey

START	Rievaulx Abbey
DISTANCE	3 miles (4.8km)
TIME	1½ hours
PARKING	Car parks at Helmsley (Pay and Display), then take seasonal bus to Rievaulx
ROUTE FEATURES	Clear tracks and paths with a short stretch along a country lane

GPS WAYPOINTS

- 🥾 SE 574 849
- Ⓐ SE 579 840
- Ⓑ SE 583 835
- Ⓒ SE 595 835

PUBLIC TRANSPORT Bus services to Helmsley, Sunday, Bank Holiday and daily summer Moorsbus service to Rievaulx

REFRESHMENTS Choice of tearooms and pubs in Helmsley, tearoom at Rievaulx Abbey

PUBLIC TOILETS Helmsley and at Rievaulx for visitors to the abbey

PLAY AREA None

ORDNANCE SURVEY MAPS Explorer OL26 (North York Moors – Western area)

🥾 From the entrance to Rievaulx Abbey, follow the lane downstream by the River Rye to a junction beside Rievaulx Bridge. Turn left below the steep escarpment of Abbot Hag Wood, but just after the lane bends left into Ingdale Howl, leave for a woodland track on the right, signed as the Cleveland Way to Helmsley Ⓐ.

The way climbs steadily through Quarry Bank Wood, later levelling below disused quarry workings that are now almost hidden by the lush vegetation. If you are not pressed for time, go left at a waymarked crossing track a little farther on Ⓑ. It leads to a field above, where grassy mounds and shallow ditches, once presumed to be the site of an abandoned medieval village are now thought to mark the sight of the monastery's original grange.

> ✳ Begun in 1132, **Rievaulx** was the first Cistercian monastery in northern England, founded by 12 monks from Clairvaux in France. Led by an English abbot, William, they faced a daunting task in clearing woodland, draining marshes, diverting rivers and constructing canals and fishponds to tame the 'vast solitude and horror', which an early writer ascribed to the valley. It took over 100 years to complete the abbey church and its attendant buildings, which, at its peak, supported 140 monks and 600 lay brothers.

Returning to **B** continue with the main track, which runs at the edge of fields above Whinny Bank Wood. At the far end, the way carries on over open ground past Griff Lodge. Keep ahead across its drive on the continuation of the Cleveland Way. Eventually, after passing through consecutive gates, the route drops steeply to negotiate a wooded valley, Blackdale Howl, climbing on the far side to emerge from the trees at the edge of expansive fields **C**.

An enclosed path takes the way on along the perimeter, in due course turning to climb around the far end. Through a kissing-gate at the top, go right onto a developing track, which gradually descends towards Helmsley. Readily spotted in the distance are the castle ruins and tower of All Saints' Church and, as you get closer, you can also see Helmsley's walled garden.

✳ Helmsley's **12th-century castle** was built primarily for defence and has imposing earthwork embankments and a spectacular ruined keep. Inside, Tudor apartments contrast with the stark military architecture, and were built when comfort later assumed a greater precedence. However, when Thomas Duncombe inherited the estate, he desired more than a draughty old castle, and in 1713, began work on a **fine new house**. Having survived two disastrous fires and 60 years as a girls' school, it has been superbly restored by the Duncombe family and is open to the public.

Ultimately the track ends by Helmsley's long-stay car park where a monument marks one end of the Cleveland Way. Turn right to explore the castle and town, or carry on ahead, past Ryeburn Teashop (which sells delicious home-made ice cream), to the end of the street, where the 13th-century church lies to the right.

If first walking from Helmsley to Rievaulx, turn left out of the vehicle entrance to the car park along the Cleveland Way. Carry on at the field edge beyond the track's end to a kissing-gate, from which an enclosed path drops left and then runs above Blackdale Howl Wood. Entering trees **C** *the path dips across a valley, emerging beyond and later crossing a drive by Griff Lodge. The Cleveland Way runs on ahead above Whinny Bank Wood, subsequently dropping through the trees and finally meeting a lane at the foot of Ingdale Howl* **A**. *Go left to Rievaulx Bridge, there turning right to the abbey.*

For those who wish to visit Rievaulx Terrace situated above the village; simply follow the ongoing lane to the main road at the top of the hill to find the entrance then on the right.

? *What is the symbol used to denote the Cleveland Way?*

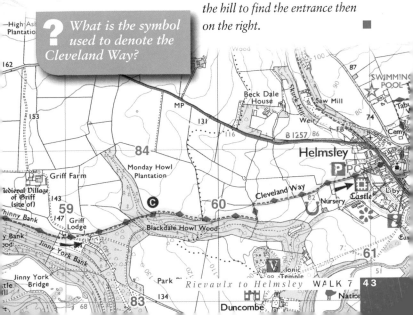

Spout House and Bilsdale

- Old inn museum
- enchanting views
- green phone box
- lovely Bilsdale

The 16th-century cruck-framed cottage that later became the original Sun Inn is the start point for this satisfying walk that follows the valley side to the tiny hamlet of Fangdale Beck. Break your journey there to wander down to the little church of St John in its pretty setting before returning above the western bank of the river.

walk 8

Overlooking Fangdale Beck

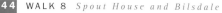

walk 8

START Sun Inn on B1257 from Helmsley

DISTANCE 3½ miles (5.6km)

TIME 1½ hours

PARKING Beside Sun Inn (no charge, but the landlord requests that you ask permission and buy some refreshment)

ROUTE FEATURES Field paths and tracks; a short stretch on the road

GPS WAYPOINTS

🖉 SE 574 935
Ⓐ SE 576 937
Ⓑ SE 576 949
Ⓒ SE 569 946
Ⓓ SE 568 934

PUBLIC TRANSPORT Sunday, Bank Holiday and daily summer Moorsbus service along Bilsdale

REFRESHMENTS Drinks only are available from the Sun Inn, but you are welcome to enjoy your own picnic at the tables outside

PUBLIC TOILETS Beside Sun Inn

PLAY AREA None

ORDNANCE SURVEY MAPS Explorer OL26 (North York Moors – Western area)

🖉 Walk up through the farmyard, bearing left through a gate beside a barn. Immediately through a second gate on the left, head across to another gate and carry on across subsequent fields, making for the buildings of Hollin Bower Farm. Over a ladder-stile Ⓐ, turn left, crossing a track to the right-hand one of two gates.

> ✴ Originally built as a farmhouse in 1550, **Spout House** served as a hostelry for 200 years until the present Sun Inn opened in 1914. Remarkably, it has survived the centuries almost unchanged and, furnished as it might have been at the close of the 19th century, gives a fascinating insight into the past.

Continue through a second gate on a faint field track footing a rising enclosure. Keep going as the track evaporates, before long coming to a stile on the left, not far from the corner. Cut right to another stile and maintain the same direction across the next rough field. Crossing back into pasture, climb beside the perimeter. Over yet another stile in the top corner, walk on to a gate, and through that, bear left to a ladder-stile. Cross the next couple of fields above Low Crossett Farm to a gate by a large sycamore. After just a few yards leave the track over a stile and pass above the buildings of High Crossett Farm to find a three-fingered signpost beneath another sycamore at the far side **B**.

Lord Feversham, the local landowner, allowed the installation of the public telephone box by the road junction into the village of **Fangdale Beck** on condition that it was painted green to harmonise with the landscape. British Telecom ran into trouble when they replaced it with a glass box in 1992, for by then it had become a listed building and the company was fined and required to reinstate it.

There, go left through a gate and past the end of the farm. Keep ahead on a track, but then immediately after a left-hand bend, turn off right to walk down-field with the hedge on your right, emerging over a stile at the bottom onto the road. Go left to find, a little way along, a path leaving on the right, which drops to a footbridge over the River Seph. Walk right into the hamlet. *However, to look at the church, instead continue a little farther along the main road past the junction.* Follow the lane up into the village to a footbridge on the left across Fangdale Beck **C**.

Turn right along a track in front of a former Methodist chapel, which soon bends left and leads to Malkin Bower Farm. Walk ahead through the farmyard, leaving by a waymarked gate. A pleasant track

Inside Spout House

leads away between the fields, later coming close above the river. Through a gate just beyond there, at a point across the valley from Spout House, turn right to climb the field edge. Turn within the top corner and continue along the valley to reach the next farm, Helm House **D**. Keep ahead to leave along a track past the farmhouse, rising to an enclosure where stone barns stand on the left. Pass through gates between them to the field behind and follow its perimeter down towards the river. Leave near the bottom corner onto a track and over a bridge, walk up to the road. Spout House is then a short walk to the left. ∎

? *What animal's head is carved on a stone cross outside the Sun Inn?*

Forge Valley and the River Derwent

- ■ Deep ravine
- ■ woodland walks
- ■ nature reserve
- ■ disabled access trail

walk 9

The deep ravine of Forge Valley is a geologically recent formation, gouged out by torrential glacial melt-waters at the end of the last Ice Age when the Derwent's original flow into the North Sea was blocked by a dam of ice near present-day Scalby. This walk wanders north from the gorge for a wonderful view of this unusual formation as the main valley splits into two.

The River Derwent at Old Man's Mouth

walk **9**

START Old Man's Mouth towards the head of Forge Valley

DISTANCE 3¾ miles (6km)

TIME 2 hours

PARKING Old Man's Mouth Car Park in Forge Valley

ROUTE FEATURES Initial steep climb; *narrow path across steep slope.* Also, 'easy going' riverside trail suitable for prams and wheelchairs

GPS WAYPOINTS
- SE 984 870
- Ⓐ SE 983 869
- Ⓑ SE 977 877
- Ⓒ SE 966 889
- Ⓓ SE 980 876

PUBLIC TRANSPORT Sunday, Bank Holiday and daily summer Moorsbus service to Forge Valley

REFRESHMENTS Pub at East Ayton 1½ miles (2.4km), picnic area beside car park

PUBLIC TOILETS None

PLAY AREA None

ORDNANCE SURVEY MAPS Explorer OL27 (North York Moors – Eastern area)

With an atmosphere heavy with smoke and echoing to the clatter of the forges that would later give it its name, the **14th-century valley** was the scene of great industrial activity. Yet it was this smelting of ironstone, using charcoal from the forest, which helped preserve the woodland. The process required great quantities of charcoal and, although there was an abundance of trees, indiscriminate felling would have rapidly exhausted them. Instead, the woodland was coppiced to produce a regular supply of small timber, and as you wander through today, you can still see the old poles of trees harvested in this way.

A footbridge, just upstream of the car park, provides a passage to a duck-boarded path along the Derwent's western bank. Go right, but after 40 yds (36m), turn off onto a permissive path, which zigzags up the steep valley side. The climb is sustained, but the track is good, and before too long levels along the upper rim of the deep valley. Just before reaching a field gate, look for a path Ⓐ that doubles back right along the top edge of Scarwell Wood.

This path leads to Spikers Hill Farm. Keep ahead behind the farm, signed towards Cockrah Foot, slipping over the second stile beyond the buildings to continue at the edge of a field. Leaving at the corner, follow a track descending along the hillside into the trees. Coming into the open, there is a splendid view along the valley. Carry on for another 20 yds (18m) to a pair of adjacent gates, beyond which is a waymarked stile **B**.

Aiming for North Stile Cottage, head on along the open meadow, skirting above a clump of trees concealing a ruined barn. Approaching the cottage, pass through a gate and climb to a stile beside it. Maintain your direction beyond, rising to join a track that ultimately leads to Cockrah House, a little less than ¾ mile (1.2km) farther on **C**.

? *What crustacean might you find living in the waters of the River Derwent?*

There, instead of following the track out over a cattle-grid, turn around to walk back along the valley, but now following the bottom edge of the field. Ignoring fishermen's stiles, stay in the pasture above the boundary, eventually reaching a stiled footbridge in a hedge and stream dropping from above. Continue briefly by the river, but as it then bends away, keep ahead across a flat apron below the slope of the hill to a gate and stile at the left end of the far fence. Soon joining a fence on your right, follow it to another stile.

Walk the length of a narrow meadow and, through a gate, bear onto higher ground above a bank of gorse. Carry on to a stile by a field gate and, maintaining height, keep going between clumps of gorse across the slope of rougher, marshy ground. Continue for some 200 yds (183m), picking your way through more gorse to find a stile in the fence rising from the left, which takes you into the Forge Valley woodland **D**.

Once into the trees, follow a descending path back to the riverbank. Head downstream along the wooden walkway, shortly returning to the bridge by the car park at Old Man's Mouth. ■

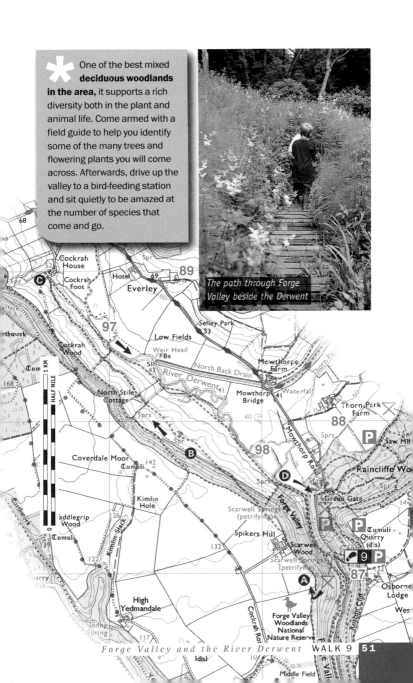

One of the best mixed **deciduous woodlands in the area,** it supports a rich diversity both in the plant and animal life. Come armed with a field guide to help you identify some of the many trees and flowering plants you will come across. Afterwards, drive up the valley to a bird-feeding station and sit quietly to be amazed at the number of species that come and go.

The path through Forge Valley beside the Derwent

Rosedale

walk 10

■ Tranquil valleys   ■ splendid views
■ attractive village   ■ site of former priory

At first sight, nothing remains of Rosedale's priory or iron mines but look again. The church contains a nun's grave and ancient stone seat, while outside stands a ruined tower; miners' cottages were built from the priory's stones, and hillsides bear muted scars from old workings. An enjoyable ramble explores the peaceful valleys that converge on the village.

Rosedale bursts into colour with the coming of spring

walk 10

START Rosedale Abbey

DISTANCE 4 miles (6.4km)

TIME 2 hours

PARKING Car parks in village

ROUTE FEATURES Field and woodland paths; moderate climbs

GPS WAYPOINTS

 SE 724 959
Ⓐ SE 723 972
Ⓑ SE 718 977
Ⓒ SE 708 976
Ⓓ SE 710 967

PUBLIC TRANSPORT Sunday, Bank Holiday and daily summer Moorsbus service to Rosedale Abbey

REFRESHMENTS Choice of pubs and cafés in the village

PUBLIC TOILETS In village

PLAY AREA None

ORDNANCE SURVEY MAPS Explorer OL26 (North York Moors – Western area)

From the junction by the Milburn Arms, take the lane to Castleton but, immediately before a bridge across Northdale Beck, turn right. Through a couple of gates, bear left, continuing above the stream. The way progresses naturally up the valley at the edge of successive fields, although not always beside the water. Carry on for some ¾ mile (1.2km) to reach a footbridge taking you across the beck Ⓐ.

On the opposite bank, ignore a footpath climbing left and instead take the bridleway through a gateway ahead. Follow a wall on your right rising above the stream until you emerge onto a lane. Cross to a gap diagonally opposite and carry on in the same direction, always gaining height across the hillside pastures. After eventually passing above a small reservoir and ruined farmstead, the way curves up to meet a track by a gate. Turn up the hill but as the gradient eases, leave right to a gate onto a lane Ⓑ.

Over a stile at a waymark 20 yds (18m) to the right, a track drops into a conifer plantation on the left. At a junction, keep ahead, the track eventually leading to a stream. The way then curves left, falling as an indistinct path through the trees. Lower down, as the stream turns away, stay ahead,

Looking along the valley towards Clough House

before long emerging over a stile by Clough House. Go right, past the front of the cottage to a field gate on the right immediately beyond. Through that bear left to join a track leading away. When you then reach a junction by a small barn, turn left and walk down to a lane by Hill Cottages **C**.

Cross to a track opposite that drops behind the houses. Keep going downhill at the edge of a large field beyond its end. Through a gate at the bottom, turn right and walk downfield to a gap in the bottom hedge. Maintain your descent across two more fields to reach a bridge over a stream in the base of the valley **D**.

Instead of crossing, follow the field boundary left and through a gate. Walk on to a stile and go left, negotiating a stream into the next field. A field track leads up to a gate. Through that, walk ahead across successive fields, eventually returning to the water's edge near

Even before the Romans arrived **Rosedale** was known for its iron-rich rock, a resource later exploited by the nearby monastic communities. With the Industrial Revolution came new demands for iron, and when a vein of high-grade ore was discovered in 1851, a major industry developed. The village's population grew four-fold to almost 3,000 people in just 20 years and by 1861, a railway was carrying the ore to the iron works in County Durham. For almost 70 years, the boom continued, but after the First World War, decline set in and the last mine closed around 1926.

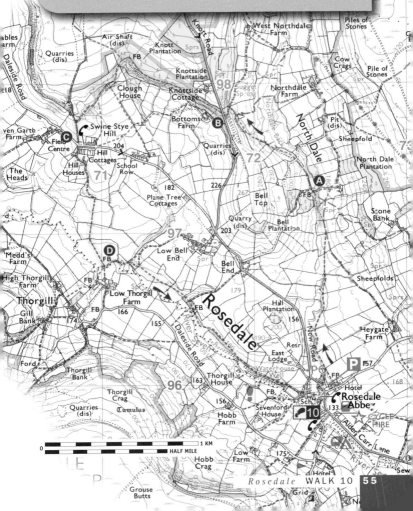

Descending into Rosedale from Swine Stye Hill

another footbridge. Again, remain on this bank and keep ahead, passing from field to field above the river and later a caravan site, before finally leaving through a kissing-gate. A drive leads on through the site. Just beyond a children's play area, signs mark a crossing footpath. Go left beside a hedge to a stile onto a lane. Turn right past the back of the church and then left at a junction to return to the village centre. ■

? What lies in the churchyard beside the east wall of the church?

Rosedale Abbey was actually a priory, founded around 1158 to house a small group of Cistercian nuns and dedicated jointly to St Mary and St Lawrence. Although it fell prey to Scottish raiders in 1322, the community actually prospered until it was dissolved in 1535 by order of King Henry VIII.

For some 300 years, the buildings were left to decay, but remained a substantial ruin until the mining boom of the 1850s. There was little thought of conservation in those days, and the ready-cut blocks of stone were plundered for building materials to be used in the rapidly expanding village of Rosedale.

Captain Cook's Monument

- **Breathtaking views**
- **picnic site**
- **landmark monument**
- **Captain Cook associations**

High on the summit of Easby Moor, commanding fantastic views over the Cleveland plain and into Kildale, is a 60-foot (18m) obelisk erected to commemorate one of England's greatest seamen, Captain James Cook. This walk to the monument meanders through the forest that cloaks the hillside upon which it stands and enjoys superb views across the surrounding countryside.

walk 11

A distant view of Roseberry Topping

START Gribdale Gate, top of Dikes Lane 1¼ miles (2km) east of Great Ayton Station

DISTANCE 4 miles (6.4km)

TIME 2 hours

PARKING At start of walk

ROUTE FEATURES Woodland paths and tracks; *very steep climb through Ayton Banks Wood*

GPS WAYPOINTS
🖉 NZ 592 109
🅐 NZ 592 104
🅑 NZ 602 103
🅒 NZ 603 100
🅓 NZ 594 097
🅔 NZ 583 103
🅕 NZ 589 101

PUBLIC TRANSPORT Rail service to Great Ayton Station 1 mile (1.6km)

REFRESHMENTS Choice of pubs and cafés in Great Ayton 2 miles (3.2km)

PUBLIC TOILETS Behind Captain Cook's Schoolhouse in Great Ayton

PLAY AREA None

ORDNANCE SURVEY MAPS Explorer OL26 (North York Moors – Western area)

Begin over a stile into the forest at the bottom of the picnic area. A rising path shortly crosses a stream before turning up more steeply beside an old wall. Meeting a track by a fenced mine shaft at the top, go left, but look out for another path leaving very soon on the right 🅐. Cresting what remains of the hill, the path then drops to a junction. Go left.

> Born to a Marton farming family in 1728, **James Cook** eventually served an apprenticeship with a sea captain from Whitby, before joining the Royal Navy. After charting the north-west Americas, Cook led an expedition to the South Seas, where he mapped New Zealand and Australia's east coast. A second circumnavigation took him to the oceans of the Antarctic, after which, he returned to the Pacific Ocean in search of a viable sea passage around the northern coast of the American continent. Tragically, he was killed by the natives of Hawaii, while trying to recover a stolen boat.

Reaching a fork, bear right with the Cleveland Way past a barrier. The path leads to a stone forest road 🅑. However, immediately before it, turn off right on a faint path, which then swings left and, becoming pronounced, slants down the hill beside a stone wall. Emerging at the bottom onto a lane, go down the hill past Bankside Farm. As it then bends at a

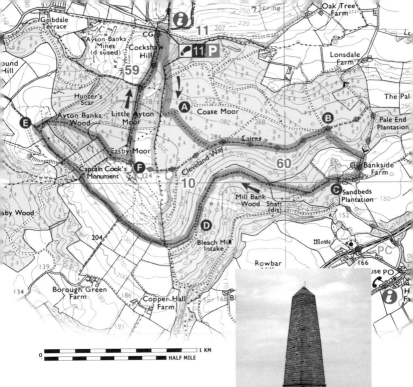

The Cook Monument

cottage, leave through a gate on the right **C** onto a climbing track signed as a bridleway.

Where it then splits, bear right, later passing a clearing from which there is a grand view into Kildale and of the more distant Cleveland Hills. At another fork **D** the waymarked bridleway keeps right, soon breaking from the trees. Through a gap, continue ahead beside a wall across the flank of Easby Moor. After almost ¾ mile (1.2km) and beyond another strip of forest, the path emerges from gorse onto open meadow where Roseberry Topping grabs your attention ahead. Watch for a fork **E**, just a little farther

? *Where and when did Captain Cook lose his life?*

Coate Moor Woods

Cook's school in nearby **Great Ayton** now houses a fascinating exhibition of his life and outstanding achievements. Have a look too at the 12th-century All Saint's Church where, in the quiet graveyard, you will find the tombstones of his mother and five of his seven brothers. To see the cottage to which his parents retired, you must visit Australia, where it was taken in 1934. But marking the spot is an obelisk, fashioned out of rock cut from Point Hicks, Cook's first landfall in Australia on April 20, 1770.

on, and branch right, rising to a gate beside a wall at the foot of Ayton Banks Wood.

Bear right, climbing among the trees to meet a broad track. Cross to the path opposite and continue very steeply up the forested hill, taking special care in wet weather for the ground can be slippery. Eventually leaving the trees behind, the gradient eases. Walk on to meet a higher path and follow it right to Captain Cook's Monument, which can now be seen directly ahead **F**.

At the monument turn sharp left on a paved path heading almost due north in the direction of the distant Roseberry Topping. As the way descends towards the forest, look for a memorial plaque on the right, which remembers the wartime crash of an RAF Lockheed Hudson in February 1940. Carry on down through the trees to return to the car park.

Nunnington

- Water mill
- country house (NT)
- medieval church
- riverside walk

Although just outside the National Park boundary, the gentle countryside around Nunnington is none the less attractive and the village has an interesting manor house to visit. Following a broad ridge, the route gives fine views to the moors in the north and the Howardian Hills to the south, before returning along the River Rye past a substantial old mill.

walk 12

Attractive cottages line the street as you climb through Nunnington

walk 12

START Caulkleys Bank, south of Nunnington

DISTANCE 4¼ miles (6.8km)

TIME 2 hours

PARKING Roadside lay-by above Caulkleys Bank

ROUTE FEATURES Field tracks and paths, moderate climb

GPS WAYPOINTS

- SE 669 782
- Ⓐ SE 689 790
- Ⓑ SE 687 793
- Ⓒ SE 675 794
- Ⓓ SE 669 793
- Ⓔ SE 665 790

PUBLIC TRANSPORT None

REFRESHMENTS Tearoom at Nunnington Hall and the Royal Oak in Nunnington village

PUBLIC TOILETS For visitors to Nunnington Hall

PLAY AREA None

ORDNANCE SURVEY MAPS Explorer OL26 (North York Moors – Western area)

Saxon farmers built the first mill here, but the present four-storey building was erected in 1875 at a cost of £700, which included the water wheel and milling machinery. It continued grinding into the 20th century and was subsequently used to generate power for Nunnington Hall until mains electricity was installed in the village in 1950.

Begin this walk along a track beside the parking area, heading east past a small copse along the top of Caulkleys Bank. Beyond a trig point, a long, gradual descent leads to a crossing track. Turn left, but then immediately fork right down another track, Caulkleys Lane. Emerging onto a lane at the bottom Ⓐ, go left to a junction and then right, signed 'Welburn' and 'Kirkbymoorside'.

Walk down past West Ness Farm towards Ness Bridge Ⓑ. Immediately before it, cross into the field on the left and carry on upstream by the River Rye at the edge of successive fields. Later reaching a fence corner, keep ahead cutting a kink in the river to a kissing-gate at the far side. Once more with the river, keep going to Mill Farm. Leaving the field, walk on through the farmyard and past the mill to a stile Ⓒ, just to the right of the farmhouse.

Nunnington's peacocks are fascinating, whatever your age

The **13th-century church** contains a fine funerary monument, once thought to represent a wandering knight, Sir Peter Loschy. Legends tell that a terrible dragon oppressed the village, and Sir Peter determined to slay it. As he hacked pieces from the beast during a hard-fought battle on nearby Loschy Hill, his dog buried them in a field above the church. The nobleman finally won the day and his faithful companion ran to lick his master's face, but the dragon's blood was poison, and both tragically died on their field of victory.

Follow the course of the mill race to a stile near the weir. Bear left across the next field to a

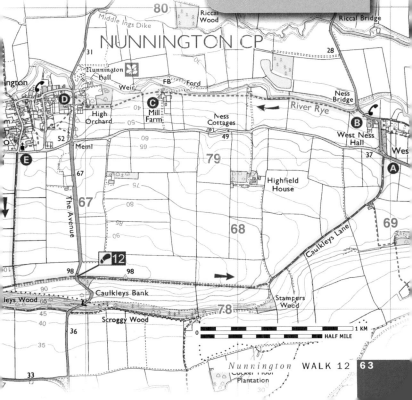

Crossing the River Rye

field gate just left of the end of a high wall surrounding Nunnington Hall. Continue beside the grounds of the house and behind a couple of estate cottages to leave the far corner of the field onto a lane **D**.

Go right, but before you reach a bridge in front of the entrance to the hall, turn left through the village. At the far end of Nunnington, the street swings left, climbing past the Royal Oak to a junction beside the church **E**. Opposite, a bridleway rises across the fields.

On reaching the crest, turn left along an avenue of Scots pine, which returns you to the parking area above Caulkleys Bank. ■

? *Where can you find mice in the Church of All Saints and St James?*

✱ Nunnington Hall dates from the Elizabethan period and was, for a time, home to the Virgin Queen's physician. It was remodelled in the 17th century and altered again in the 1920s. The walled garden is a rare survival from the 17th-century walled garden and the orchard, where peacocks roam contains old varieties of apple tree. Inside many of the furnishings reflect its last owners, the Fifes, who gave the property to the National Trust in 1952. But the highlight for any visitor young or old is the Carlisle Collection, a display of beautifully crafted miniature rooms, each furnished in exquisite detail to represent a different period.

Staithes

■ **Delightful village** ■ **heritage centre**
■ **dramatic cliff walk** ■ **nature reserve**

From the narrow, twisting stone streets of picturesque Staithes, this walk follows the coast south east to Port Mulgrave. The return lies through a pretty woodland nature reserve, rich in wild flowers and birds, before leading back to the old village, where Cook developed his passion for the sea while working in William Sanderson's haberdashery and grocery shop.

Small boats lie in the creek behind the harbour

walk 13

START Staithes

DISTANCE 4½ miles (7.2km)

TIME 2 hours

PARKING Car park above old village (Pay and Display)

ROUTE FEATURES Field and woodland paths; *sustained climb; exposed cliffs*

GPS WAYPOINTS
- NZ 780 184
- Ⓐ NZ 783 188
- Ⓑ NZ 792 183
- Ⓒ NZ 794 173
- Ⓓ NZ 791 170
- Ⓔ NZ 784 166
- Ⓕ NZ 776 179

PUBLIC TRANSPORT Bus service to Staithes

REFRESHMENTS Choice of pubs in Staithes and Fox and Hounds at Dalehouse

PUBLIC TOILETS Adjacent to car park

PLAY AREA None

ORDNANCE SURVEY MAPS Explorer OL27 (North York Moors – Eastern area)

With tiny cottages perched on the cliffs like nests in a seabird colony, it is hardly surprising that little room has been left in the old village for its streets. In fact, Dog Loup claims the title for the narrowest street in northern England. Until the advent of the steam trawler, **Staithes** lived by fishing, and in the 19th century, there were some 300 men sailing from here in small cobles, their catches being among the largest along the coast.

Leaving the car park, follow the main street down to the old village. At the bottom, where High Street swings right, it is worth detouring left to a bridge across the foot of Staithes Beck. Go left, climbing Cowbar Bank, leaving when it then swings sharply left, over a stile on the right. A path leads onto the headland of Cowbar Nab from which there is a stunning view across to the village.

Returning to the High Street, follow it on to the Cod and Lobster by the harbour Ⓐ. Turn up Church Street, passing Cook's Cottage and a small mission church. Continue with the Cleveland Way, watching for the path swinging left at a sign to Runswick Bay. Beyond farm buildings, keep ahead across successive fields, eventually rising to a final gate at the cliff top Ⓑ.

Carry on at the field edge above grassy cliffs, climbing gently to the high point by Beacon Hill. Beyond, the way

? *To whom is the small mission church in Staithes dedicated?*

descends easily towards Port Mulgrave. Over a stile, continue along a narrow lane past cottages above the old harbour before turning from the coast.

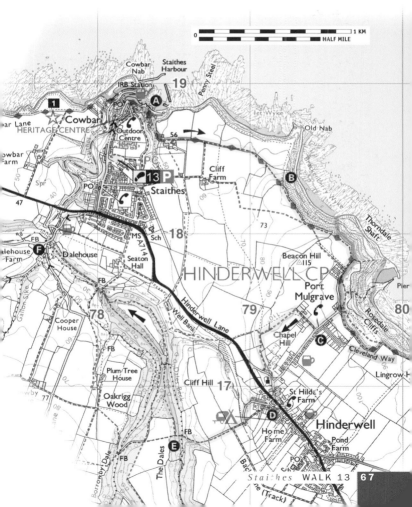

When you reach a telephone box **C**, turn right towards a farm, progressing into a field at the end of the track. At a fingerpost walk left joining a hedge to reach a stile in the corner. Carry on beside a fence, swinging left around its corner and passing a redundant stile. Over a stile at the end, drop through trees to emerge onto a lane by St Hilda's Church. Follow it left to the main road **D**.

Cross into West End Close opposite and, at the bottom, walk right along Porret Lane, which then degrades to a track. At a

Staithes

house, go right on a track. Where that turns left, continue ahead at the edge of a field and on over stiles, soon falling into a wooded gully. Across a stream at the bottom, scale the opposite bank, emerging from the trees into an open field **E**.

Turn right along its perimeter, returning to the trees in the corner. Go left and then almost immediately right on a path that gradually descends along the

The village overlocks the narrow creek of Staithes Beck

crest of a narrowing ridge. At a junction, walk ahead to follow the left flank. Leaving the trees, the way continues as a broad grassy swathe before losing height to a bridge by a small caravan site. A track leads away beside the stream to the hamlet of Dalehouse **F**.

Turn right past the Fox and Hounds, rising beyond to a junction with the main road. Go right again, using the pedestrian crossing to reach the side road back into Staithes.

Iron-rich cliffs overlooking a convenient landing brought industry to **Port Mulgrave** in the 1850s, and a harbour was completed in 1857, enabling the ore to be shipped to Tyneside. After the deposits were exhausted, a mile-long (1.6km) tunnel was dug through the cliffs for a mineral railway, connecting the port with iron mines at nearby Easington. But when these closed in 1930, the railway was dismantled, and following the outbreak of war, to prevent its use by invading German forces, the harbour pier was partly demolished.

Robin Hood's Bay

- Fossil beach
- heritage museum
- spectacular cliff walk
- stunning coastal views

walk 14

Described by Arthur Mee as one of the most astonishing sights along the Yorkshire coast, Robin Hood's Bay has long been popular with holidaymakers and walkers, and marks the end of the famous 'Coast to Coast' walk, that begins at St Bees Head in Cumbria. After following the cliffs, the route returns along the former coastal railway between Whitby and Scarborough.

Robin Hood's Bay marks the end of the Coast to Coast walk

walk 14

START Robin Hood's Bay, above old town

DISTANCE 4¾ miles (7.6km)

TIME 2¼ hours

PARKING Station Car Park (Pay and Display)

ROUTE FEATURES Coast path and disused railway line; unfenced cliffs; moderate climb

GPS WAYPOINTS

🖊 NZ 950 054
Ⓐ NZ 952 070
Ⓑ NZ 944 080
Ⓒ NZ 942 074

PUBLIC TRANSPORT Bus service to Robin Hood's Bay

REFRESHMENTS Choice of pubs and cafés in Robin Hood's Bay

PUBLIC TOILETS Adjacent to car park

PLAY AREA None

ORDNANCE SURVEY MAPS Explorer OL27 (North York Moors – Eastern area)

The Bay Hotel overlooks the slipway

🖊 Begin along Mount Pleasant North, which is signed 'Cleveland Way' and leaves the main road almost opposite Station Car Park. Where it bends left at the end, keep ahead through a gate in front of houses to Rocket Post Field. The way continues around its perimeter and on above the cliffs, giving views of the sweeping coastline to the north and south.

In due course, the path passes the foot of Rain Dale, where twin gullies bring streams to cascade over the precipitous edge. *A concessionary path Ⓐ to the abandoned railway climbs the ridge that separates them, providing a convenient link to the return route if you wish to shorten the walk.* Otherwise, keep going above the sheer cliffs, which, ahead, rise to the highest point along the coastal section of this walk. The onward route is never in doubt, eventually dipping sharply to cross a stream by a National Trust marker 'Bottom House Farm'.

Over the stream, leave the cliffs along the Centenary Path **B**, which rises beside a wall above Limekiln Slack. Mounting a stile, continue up the next field to leave from its top-right corner **C**. Now on the trackbed of the old railway, turn left and follow it back to Robin Hood's Bay, an easy stroll of some 1¾ miles (2.8km). Through a gate at its end, bear left into Mount Pleasant North to return to the car park.

No one really knows how the legendary **Robin Hood** became associated with this little fishing village; one of the few safe landings along the rocky and treacherous coast and which grew to prominence during the mid-16th century. Tales tell of him assisting the Abbot of Whitby repel Scandinavian raiders or giving help to the villagers who offered him a refuge from the law. But what is certain is that the place grew rich, not just from fishing, but by smuggling. The contraband was hidden in a network of secret tunnels and passages after being furtively shipped from France and the Low Countries.

The Rocket Post

Leave your vehicle in the car park while you wander down to explore the lower town and its expansive beach. Children will enjoy investigating the many rock pools exposed at low tide, and, if lucky, will find fossil ammonites and belemnites among the rocks washed out from the crumbling cliffs. *But, watch for rock falls, an ever-present danger, and incoming tides, which can cut off your retreat.* ■

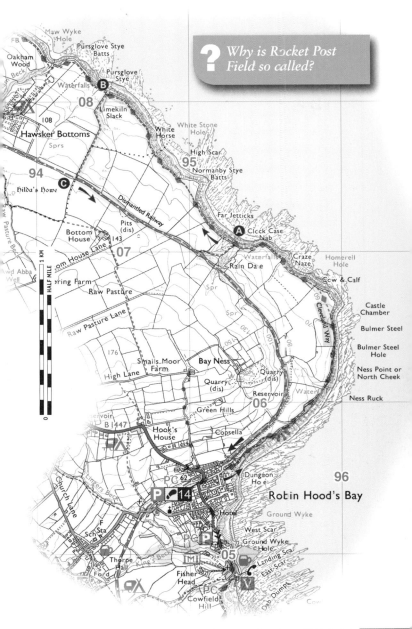

? *Why is Rocket Post Field so called?*

Hutton-le-Hole
and Lastingham

■ **Folk museum**   ■ **pretty villages**
■ **11th-century crypt**   ■ **moorland views**

walk 15

Yorkshire has any number of captivating villages, but Hutton-le-Hole must be rated among the most charming; ancient cottages are set behind rolling greens where sheep graze above a babbling stream. This pleasant walk crosses the fields to nearby Lastingham where the church has a beautiful crypt, beneath which lie the bones of one of the early Celtic missionaries, St Cedd.

On the path to Spaunton

walk 15

START Hutton le Hole

DISTANCE 5 miles (8km)

TIME 2½ hours

PARKING Car park at edge of village (fee)

ROUTE FEATURES Field paths and tracks, with short section on lane; *steep climb*

GPS WAYPOINTS

SE 705 902
Ⓐ SE 706 896
Ⓑ SE 711 898
Ⓒ SE 723 899
Ⓓ SE 729 904
Ⓔ SE 721 903

PUBLIC TRANSPORT Sunday, Bank Holiday and daily summer Moorsbus service to Hutton-le-Hole

REFRESHMENTS Inn and teashops at Hutton-le-Hole and Blacksmiths Arms in Lastingham

PUBLIC TOILETS Adjacent to car park

PLAY AREA None

ORDNANCE SURVEY MAPS Explorer OL26 (North York Moors – Western area)

From the car park, turn left and then left again down the main street. Continue to a junction beyond a bridge at the edge of the village Ⓐ and go left. After 50 yds (46m), fork left onto a track, marked as a bridleway to Cropton, bearing left again where that shortly divides. The way climbs steadily along the course of an ancient, banked track.

At the top Ⓑ, the track bends left and right around the edge of a field, to head almost due east for nearly ½ mile (800m) over the crest of the hill. Eventually swinging left and then right by barns, it leads to Grange Farm. Leave the fields and wind between barns to emerge onto a lane. Just to the right at a junction Ⓒ, turn left to walk through Spaunton, in due course dropping to another junction beyond the village.

Go right, but then immediately leave onto a waymarked path on the left. Through a gate, it descends a wooded gully, meeting a track at the bottom, which leads into Lastingham. Keep ahead past cottages overlooking a stream and, after crossing a bridge, turn left. At the next junction Ⓓ, by a telephone box, go left again to St Mary's Church.

Return to the junction by the telephone box Ⓓ and turn left, climbing out of the village

One of Lastingham's delightful cottage gardens

and, through a gate at the top, onto the moor. Reaching a stone cross, a little farther on, go left towards High Cross, following a wall downhill. Carry on and, over a brook, continue by the wall up the opposite bank. Where it ends, keep ahead across moorland to join a track guiding you away from Camomile Farm. It shortly curves to the left, eventually emerging onto a lane **E**.

✳ The first church at **Lastingham** was built in 654, when St Cedd, invited by King Ethelwald, came from Holy Island off the Northumbrian coast to found a new monastic community here. He eventually became a bishop, but died of plague in 664. St Mary's marks the site of the early monastery, and was begun in 1078 when Stephen, formerly Abbot of Whitby, re-founded the community under the Benedictine Order. The crypt is unique in this country, having a nave, aisles and chancel, and its wonderful atmosphere is full of peace and spirituality.

❓ *Can you find two wells in Lastingham dedicated to the saints associated with the monastery?*

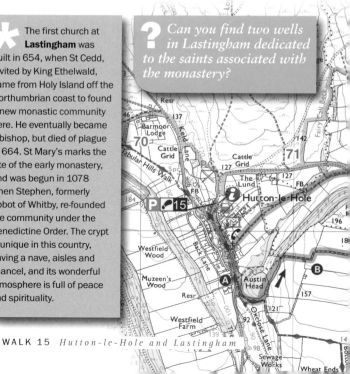

Follow the lane right for ½ mile (800m), leaving at a waymark onto a track that rises on the left above the road and soon leads to a gate into a small wood. A descending path re-crosses Fairy Call Beck at the bottom, leading to a field beyond. Keep walking ahead across a succession of fields, finally winding around Hutton's bowling green and beside the churchyard to return to the village. The car park lies to the right, beyond the folk museum. ■

Make time to visit Hutton's **open-air folk museum**, where more than a dozen historic buildings have been rebuilt, rescued from the surrounding area. From humble cruck-frame cottages, to an Elizabethan manor house, the collection includes a village shop, blacksmith's forge and work-sheds. There is even a Victorian photographer's studio to explore. Together with many other fascinating exhibits, they portray aspects of moor and dale life over the centuries, showing how people earned their living, with regular demonstrations of traditional crafts and activities.

Byland Abbey

- woodland
- country pub
- Cistercian abbey
- attractive countryside

Following part of the National Park boundary, this walk wanders across open fields to the spectacular ruins of Byland Abbey, returning through Wass and the woodland above the village. The nearby abbey at Ampleforth was founded in 1802 under the Benedictine Order, and the late Cardinal Hulme was among those who have studied and worked there.

walk 16

Byland Abbey from afar

START Jerry Carr Bank,
west of Ampleforth

DISTANCE 5 miles (8km)

TIME 2½ hours

PARKING Roadside lay-by
beside Carr Lane

ROUTE FEATURES Field and
woodland paths with
sustained ascents

GPS WAYPOINTS
🥾 SE 573 786
Ⓐ SE 563 783
Ⓑ SE 553 782
Ⓒ SE 550 790
Ⓓ SE 554 793
Ⓔ SE 560 803
Ⓕ SE 564 791

PUBLIC TRANSPORT
Sunday, Bank Holiday and
daily summer Moorsbus
service to Byland Abbey
(Alternative Start)

REFRESHMENTS Wombwell
Arms at Wass

PUBLIC TOILETS Behind
Abbey Inn for visitors to
abbey

PLAY AREA None

ORDNANCE SURVEY MAPS
Explorer OL26 (North York
Moors – Western area)

🥾 At a waymark, a short way downhill
from the lay-by, turn into the field on the
left. Follow a diagonal route signed to
Byland and Colley Broach Road,
maintaining your direction across
subsequent fields to reach a footbridge.
Now bear right to the top corner and then
diagonally left over the swell of a hill. Head
down to a stile and gate, just left of a pond,
from which a grass track leads on towards
Wass Grange.

Entering a field by the farm Ⓐ, leave the
track. Walk across to the opposite boundary
and turn left, continuing beyond the corner
to a power-line post on the hillside. There
bear right, the overhead cables guiding you
to a stile. Less than 100 yds (91m) along
pass through the hedge on the left. Go right
and then strike left across the field to a stile.
A sign to Byland Abbey directs you up the
field edge, the ruins appearing as you crest
the rise. Reaching the scant ruins of a barn
Ⓑ, turn right and walk downfield.

Through a gate, carry on beside an
outgrown hedge, ignoring a wire fence stile
and gap through it, just a short distance
along. At a waymark farther on, slip
through a break and continue on its
opposite flank. As the imposing west wall
of the abbey comes into view, go through

an opening in the end hedge to reach the abbey's perimeter fence. Turn right, pass a redundant stile and carry on beyond the corner to emerge over a final stile onto a lane  **C**.

The abbey entrance lies to the left, but return to this point after visiting to resume the walk, continuing along the drive opposite to Abbey House Farm. Just a few paces along, cross a stile into a paddock on the right. Make for another stile on the far side and then bear left to a kissing-gate at the far, top corner by Abbey Bank Wood. Keep going across two more fields to reach a lane. Turn right into Wass. At a junction by the Wombwell Arms **D**, go left up Wass Bank.

Beautiful patterned floor tiles are one of the abbey's distinctive features

Opposite the last house on the right (Wass Bank), take an unmarked path on the left, which drops to a footbridge over a brook. Bear right up the bank into forest to join a broader path, climbing parallel with the lane. Narrowing higher up, it curves left to tackle a steeper rise. Leave there for a less distinct path on the right, which drops over the shoulder of the hill back to the stream. Cross on a culvert and climb beyond to emerge back onto the lane. Carry on up the hill for another ¼ mile (400m), but just before the gradient eases, turn off right **E** onto a track that meanders across the fields to a house. There, pass through a gate into the field on the left.

Follow the right-hand fence down to a stile at the corner from which a winding path continues through woodland. Appearing from the trees, head right down to High Woods Farm and go right at the bottom along the field above Low Wood. After

Byland Abbey was founded in 1177 by 12 Cistercian monks, who had left Furness Abbey in Lancashire some 40 years before in search of a new home. Its spiritual reputation flourished and the monastic house soon became known as one of the 'three luminaries of the north'. At its peak during the 13th century, it supported a community of 36 monks and 100 lay brethren.

The fringes of Abbey Wood

crossing two fence lines, bear left away from the faint track, to find a stile at the far-left corner of the enclosure **F**.

White spots on the trunks mark an otherwise indistinct path descending through the trees. Leaving the wood, walk down to a footbridge in the left hedge and continue up the field beyond. Stiles take the way over a crossing track leading to Carr House, which then rises to another stile. The route follows the field edge below a wood to a footbridge. Now bear right, exiting at the distant bottom corner onto Carr Lane. The lay-by from which you began lies a short distance up the hill.

? *What was used to pave the floor of the great abbey church?*

Hole of Horcum

■ Steam railway
■ dramatic views
■ smugglers' inn
■ stunning moorland

As well as stunning scenery, the North York Moors has one of the finest steam railways in the country. This ramble brings them together, linking Newton Dale Halt and Levisham Station by a route through one of the Moor's most spectacular natural features. Take the first morning train from either Pickering or Grosmont to ensure you have ample time.

walk 17

Levisham Station marks the end of the walk

walk 17

START Newton Dale Halt

DISTANCE 5¼ miles (8.4km)

TIME 2½ hours

PARKING Car parks at both Pickering and Grosmont (Pay and Display), take train to Newton Dale Halt (check return times from Levisham Station)

ROUTE FEATURES Moorland paths and steep climbs; *unguarded cliff edge*

GPS WAYPOINTS

 SE 834 948
Ⓐ SE 838 946
Ⓑ SE 851 943
Ⓒ SE 849 940
Ⓓ SE 838 918
Ⓔ SE 828 918

PUBLIC TRANSPORT Bus service to Pickering, main line rail service to Grosmont

REFRESHMENTS None

PUBLIC TOILETS None en route

PLAY AREA None

ORDNANCE SURVEY MAPS Explorer OL27 (North York Moors – Eastern area)

 Leave the station at Newton Dale Halt and, beneath the railway bridge, turn left to follow Pickering Beck upstream below the embankment. Reaching a bridge, cross the stream and head away by a fence at the edge of Pifelhead Wood. A stile higher up takes the way onto the opposite side of the fence to continue into a narrowing gully. Steps ease the way up the steepest stretch, but the ascent is soon completed, and quite suddenly ends through a gate at Hudson's Cross on the moor above **Ⓐ**.

As you then go left above Yewtree Scar, there is a magnificent view into Newton Dale. Proceed beside a fence farther on to arrive at a wall and there bear right, following it away from the cliffs towards buildings visible in the middle distance. Where the wall later ends, strike right and

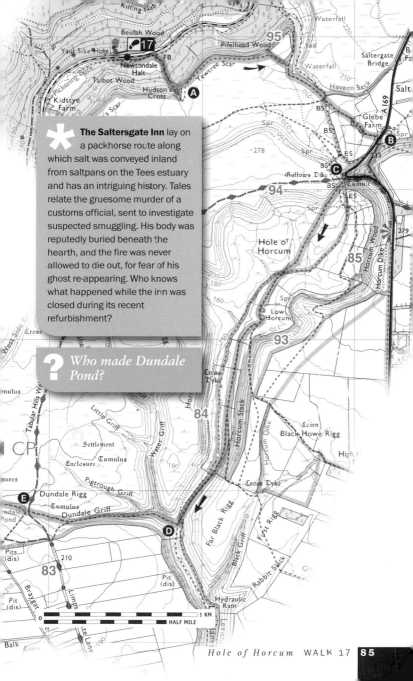

The Saltersgate Inn lay on a packhorse route along which salt was conveyed inland from saltpans on the Tees estuary and has an intriguing history. Tales relate the gruesome murder of a customs official, sent to investigate suspected smuggling. His body was reputedly buried beneath the hearth, and the fire was never allowed to die out, for fear of his ghost re-appearing. Who knows what happened while the inn was closed during its recent refurbishment?

? *Who made Dundale Pond?*

Walking through Pifelhead Wood by Newton Dale Halt

then fork left above the shallowing valley of Havern Beck, shortly reaching a stile by a gate. Wander on towards Glebe Farm and, over a couple more stiles, leave past it along a track, which joins the main road beside the 'Legendary Saltersgate Inn' **B**.

The railway from Whitby to Pickering opened in 1836 and was one of the country's earliest lines. Engineered by **George Stephenson**, it was designed originally for horse-drawn carriages, which looked more like stagecoaches than railway carriages. Above Beck Hole, carriages were hauled up an incline, but once over the watershed, they freewheeled down Newton Dale, reportedly reaching speeds of 30 miles (48km) per hour. The line was an immediate success and within 11 years, had been converted to steam. It closed in 1965, but, thanks to the hard work of dedicated enthusiasts, regular services resumed in 1973.

Across the carriageway to the right, a path rises through a gate to climb steeply through a conifer plantation above the road. Appearing from the trees at the top, walk out to rejoin the main road. Cross to find a path running below the verge from which there is a stunning view across the Hole of Horcum. Follow it right down to a hairpin bend. Approaching a gate, drop to a ladder-stile on the left **C**, from which a path descends into the Hole.

Continue through a gate and on below an isolated cottage, Low Horcum. Beyond there, bear away from the path that rises towards the woodland and carry on across the open pastures beneath the bank. Farther on, where the track again heads into the wood, keep right on the grassy swathe to a gate. The valley then narrows, the path progressing along a steepening slope above the wooded stream, eventually, falling to a footbridge **D**.

Walk on to cross a second stream and then turn right at a signpost to Dundale Pond beside the tributary stream into Dundale Griff. The path rises easily along the base of the wooded valley, later emerging onto heather moor. When you reach a fork, bear right to remain in the shallow depression that is the head of the valley, making for a signpost, which comes into view just below the skyline.

This spectacularly massive **amphitheatre**, some 300 feet (91m) deep, was created at the end of the Ice Age by torrential melt-waters carrying debris released by the retreating ice. Its striking appearance has given rise to all manner of legends as to the Hole's creation, one attributing it to a local giant called Wade, who, enraged over some domestic matter, scooped up a handful of earth and threw it at his rigglesome wife.

At the junction **E**, the path ahead is signed to Levisham Station and takes you past Dundale Pond, before long reaching another junction by the corner of a wall. Again go forward, with the wall on your left, and beyond its end, continue to the lip of an abrupt bank above Newton Dale. A sloping track leads left to the road below, where you can cut across its hairpin bend before following it down to Levisham Station. ■

The vast amphitheatre of the Hole of Horcum

Mallyan Spout

- Dramatic waterfall
- steam railway
- attractive village
- *Heartbeat* countryside

Better known to Heartbeat *fans as Aidensfield, Goathland is set within a widening of a deep rift splitting the upper moors, with bare, steep-sided hills falling to a rich motley of pasture and woodland. The North Yorkshire Moors Railway and the famous Mallyan Spout add to its undoubted appeal and are all visited on this grand promenade.*

walk 18

Goathland Station

walk **18**

START Goathland

DISTANCE $5\frac{1}{4}$ miles (8.4km)

TIME $2\frac{1}{2}$ hours

PARKING Car parks in village centre (Pay and Display)

ROUTE FEATURES Moor and woodland paths; moderate climbs

GPS WAYPOINTS

📝 NZ 833 013
Ⓐ NZ 837 013
Ⓑ NZ 835 022
Ⓒ NZ 821 021
Ⓓ NZ 824 011
Ⓔ NZ 827 007

PUBLIC TRANSPORT Bus and rail services

REFRESHMENTS Choice of pubs and tearooms at Goathland, Warehouse Tea Room at Station, Birch Hall pub at Beck Hole

PUBLIC TOILETS Beside car park

PLAY AREA None

ORDNANCE SURVEY MAPS Explorer OL27 (North York Moors – Eastern area)

Today's **North Yorkshire Moors Railway** was part of a route to Rillington, built to open the hinterland to the port at Whitby. From 6,000 passengers in its inaugural year, well over a quarter of a million now ride the steam and occasional heritage diesel services that stop at **Goathland**, where the station has a 1920s country look. As well as doubling as Aidensfield, it shot to even greater fame after appearing as Hogsmeade in the first *Harry Potter* film.

📝 Leaving the car park go right and then left through the village, keeping ahead on the bend to the station. Carefully cross the line, making sure that you close the gates behind Ⓐ and take the path climbing left,

? *What is the penalty for not shutting the crossing gate at Goathland Station?*

signed to Darnholm. It follows the rim of the valley, later plunging into a striking amphitheatre gouged from the hillside. At the bottom, the path veers to a footbridge and continues across nibbled turf to another bridge at the far side. Emerging onto a lane Ⓑ, go right to cross Eller Beck, bearing left as the track then divides.

Over a footbridge, tackle the steep hillside to a gate just beyond the crest. Through

Darnholm

that, follow the left wall and join a track. Keep ahead past a cottage and through another gate onto bracken hillside. Where the path splits, stay high by the wall, but, at a waymarked fork just a little farther on, slant downhill, going straight over a waymarked crossing part-way down. Breaking free of the bracken, the path becomes indistinct, but maintain your line towards Hill Farm, the collection of buildings ahead.

Its track drops to a lane, which, over the bridge, winds through Beck Hole. Just past the Birch Hall **C**, turn right onto a gated bridleway that curves left to Incline Cottage. Across the grass opposite, a gated path is signed to Mallyan. Beyond a couple of fields it climbs steeply into wood, dropping more easily and eventually leading to a junction beside West Beck **D**.

The spectacular waterfall of Mallyan Spout lies just ahead, but *the last section is bouldery and requires care. Do not attempt it if the*

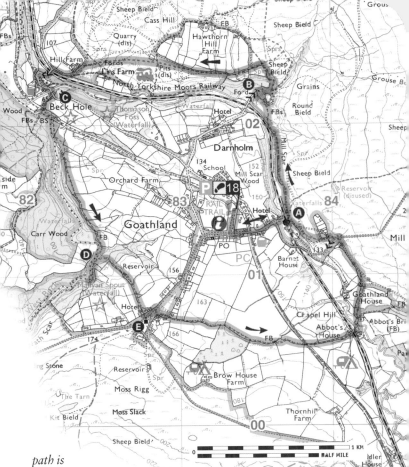

*path is
flooded.* The dramatic
path wanders through the gorge
for another ¾ mile (1.2km), but
you should return to **D** to
continue the walk.

Now take the path to
Goathland, which climbs
determinedly to emerge beside

With the arrival of the
railway, **Beck Hole** grew as
a mining village supplying the iron
works of Teesside and, in the 19th
century, there were two blast
furnaces to process ore dug from
the hillside. The mines closed in the
1880s and only a handful of the old
miners' cottages remain.

The dramatic fall of Mallyan Spout

the Mallyan Spout Hotel **E**. Go left, but after 50 yds (46m) turn right on a track to Abbot's House. Pass through the right-hand gate at the end, continuing at the edge of successive meadows. Towards the far end of the third field, look for a slab bridging a brook. Go left to a stile into a small camping field and turn right, emerging at a junction.

Keep ahead, soon passing beneath the railway at Abbot's House Farm. Go left before the buildings to cross Eller Beck by a footbridge. Carry on through a gate and over a brook, then bear left to climb beside a fence. Over a stile at the top, continue at the edge of bracken, maintaining direction to a lane at the top. Walk left.

Reaching the main road, turn left and immediately right along a drive, branching left just before a cattle-grid onto a swathe. At a fork, bear left again down the slope to find a lower path along the bank top above the railway. Follow it right until you reach a bench then, sticking with the wall, drop to the gate at the station, through which you began the walk. ■

Ravenscar

- Old alum works
- Coastal Centre (NT)
- splendid moorland
- great coastal views

Although quite a long walk, setting out from the coast to cross the open moor before returning along the course of the former Whitby to Scarborough railway and passing the site of abandoned alum workings, the route is not difficult and any effort is well rewarded by splendid coastal views.

walk 19

Along the coast to Robin Hood's Bay

walk **19**

START Ravenscar

DISTANCE 6½ miles (10.5km)

TIME 3 hours

PARKING Roadside parking by Coastal Centre

ROUTE FEATURES Moorland tracks and disused railway line; moderate climbs

GPS WAYPOINTS
- 🔲 NZ 979 015
- Ⓐ NZ 976 012
- Ⓑ NZ 970 012
- Ⓒ NZ 944 006
- Ⓓ NZ 951 017
- Ⓔ NZ 953 024
- Ⓕ NZ 968 018
- Ⓖ NZ 975 015

PUBLIC TRANSPORT Bus service to Ravenscar

REFRESHMENTS Bar snacks and meals at Raven Hall Hotel and Ravenscar Tea Rooms on Station Road, drinks at Coastal Centre

PUBLIC TOILETS At start of walk

PLAY AREA None

ORDNANCE SURVEY MAPS Explorer OL27 (North York Moors – Eastern area)

👣 Follow a descending track from the National Trust Coastal Centre, which is signed as the Cleveland Way. Shortly reaching a fork, bear right walking to another junction some 200 yds (193m) farther on. Now double back left and climb to a bridge over the old railway track. Carry on for another 50 yds (46m) and turn sharp right through a gate into a rough field.

✳ Wide streets and isolated grand houses suggest **Ravenscar** is not all it might seem. In 1895, led by John Septimus Bland and encouraged by the success of the new railway, a consortium of Yorkshire businessmen planned a fashionable resort. Centred on a square by the railway station, they laid out streets and drains to serve some 1,200 houses. Perhaps because of the bleak, windswept location or the lack of an attractive beach, the scheme failed to catch the public imagination and few buildings were ever built.

Head up towards a cottage, leaving through a gate onto its drive. Follow the drive up and then left, walking out to reach a lane **A**.

Turn right, continuing beyond a farm on a track. After 50 yds (46m), cross a waymarked stile on the left and head steeply up the hill to find a gate and stile at the top right corner. Go left at the edge of heath to emerge onto a lane beside a transmitter mast. Almost opposite, a waymarked bridleway **B** leads away across the open moor. After ¾ mile (1.2km), the track forks, the left branch avoiding a very boggy area a short way ahead. The paths meet beyond it but then immediately split again. Continue along the right branch, which is still marked as a bridleway. The path now falls more noticeably, eventually ending at a junction in front of a farm at Cook House **C**.

Low Peak Alum Works

A concrete track is signed right to How Dale and follows the edge of the moor back towards the coast. Ignore the turnings off to the left, but notice two low mounds in the adjacent fields, which are burial barrows. Eventually the track winds down into a yard behind Howdale Farm **D**.

? What was used to defend the Alum Works against raiding pirates?

Following a sign to How Dale, walk at the side of the yard to find a stile to the left of the barn. Stay by the right-hand perimeter of a rough field below the farmhouse, leaving through a gate onto its access track. Accompany it downhill for some 200 yds (183m) and, as overhead cables cross the track,

✳ Raven Hall was built in 1774, the country mansion of Captain William Childs who owned the alum quarries. A later owner, Dr Francis Willis rose to fame as physician to Europe's royalty, and treated King George III when he developed his 'madness', possibly in this very house. Since 1895 it has been run as an hotel, its rooms and terraces enjoying grand views of the coast.

turn right onto a narrow path dropping steeply through the trees to a bridge over a stream at the bottom. In the field beyond, climb ahead to a waymark and then bear left to a stile. Keep going through trees and then across a shale bank to a cottage, the former How Dale School. Follow a track away, for 250 yds (239m) to a junction, there turning left down to Browside Farm. Bear left behind the buildings to join the old railway track **E**.

Turn right and enjoy the easy walk above the coast. After 1 mile (1.6km), look for a path leaving over a stile on the left **F**. A trod falls purposefully across unkempt pasture, emerging over a stile beside a gate at the bottom onto another track, the Cleveland Way. Follow it right, passing a drive to a lone house, just beyond which a path is signed off on the left to the ruins of the Low Peak Alum Works.

> A necessary chemical in tanning and dyeing as well as being used in the manufacture of candles and parchment, **alum** was discovered in the North Yorkshire shales, and Ravenscar was one of some 30 places along the coast where it was dug. Quarrying began in 1640 and the factory above the cliffs was built to extract the salt. The industry collapsed when an alternative source was discovered, involving the treatment of colliery waste with sulphuric acid, and the works closed in 1862.

Return to the Cleveland Way and go left, very shortly branching right to climb through a sycamore wood. Reaching another junction at the top **G**, the way back is to the left, soon picking up your outward track back to the Coastal Centre.

*However, you might first detour to have a look at the site of the Ravenscar Brick Works, which is signposted from **G** to the right. The path runs below the embankment of the old railway, soon turning beneath it. Immediately beyond go right to find the brick works a short distance beyond, on the left of the track.* ■

Farndale

- **Stunning views**
- **pretty hamlets**
- **evocative moorland**
- **unspoilt valleys**

walk **20**

During early April, Farndale's open woodland beside the winding Dove is resplendent with a carpet of yellow, as countless daffodils burst into flower. But at any other season, it is still a wonderful place, and makes a fitting end to this longer, but not too demanding walk, that explores the heather moor of Rudland Rigg, where you will often hear the gabbling calls of the red grouse.

Low Mill

walk 20

START Low Mill, Farndale

DISTANCE 6½ miles (10.5km)

TIME 3 hours

PARKING Car park at Low Mill (charge)

ROUTE FEATURES Field paths and moorland tracks, sustained but moderate climb

GPS WAYPOINTS
- ✎ SE 672 952
- Ⓐ SE 657 959
- Ⓑ SE 640 974
- Ⓒ SE 661 971
- Ⓓ SE 668 970

PUBLIC TRANSPORT Sunday and Bank Holiday Moorsbus service to Farndale during April

REFRESHMENTS Seasonal café at High Mill and pub near route at Church Houses

PUBLIC TOILETS At car park

PLAY AREA None

ORDNANCE SURVEY MAPS Explorer OL26 (North York Moors – Western area)

✎ Turn right out of the car park and follow the lane north up the valley. After ¼ mile (400m), leave through a gate on the left, along a track signed as a bridleway to Rudland Rigg. Reaching a junction at Horn End Farm, walk ahead, the track taking you into the fields beyond. Keep going through successive gates, the route taking you into West Gill below Horn Ridge. Beyond the ruin of High Barn, the way bears left to West Gill Beck. Carry on above it to find a bridge across Ⓐ.

Climb away beside a wall, crossing it by a stile higher up. Continue on a faint path diverging from the wall, rising to a signpost. There go right, gaining height to a gate in the upper wall. Walk on beyond, steadily rising towards the head of the valley. After some ¾ mile (1.2km), pass a

> ✳ Now protected within a nature reserve that was created in 1953, **Farndale's wild daffodils** have heralded spring in the valley for centuries, and are known locally as 'Lenten Lilies', since their flowering often coincides with Easter. Until the 16th century, wild daffodils were common in woodlands throughout the country, although local stories attribute these to being planted either by the monks of Rievaulx Abbey or to the martyr, Nicholas Postgate, a 17th-century Catholic priest who was brutally executed for baptising a baby.

✳ Bleak, windswept moors and isolated valleys emphasise the elemental forces of nature, and it is hardly surprising that beliefs in the **supernatural** and the 'other world' have been strong in these tightly-knit dale communities. Stories of hobgoblins abound, the little people who emerge under the cover of darkness to work mischief or provide help as they saw befitting the behaviour of their mortal companions. A tale tells of Obtrusch, who lived on **Rudland Rigg** and so plagued one of Farndale's farmers that he was forced to pack his few belongings on a cart and abandon his farmstead to escape the vindictive tormentor. 'Ah see thoo's flittin' called a neighbour as he left, but the farmer turned pale as he heard a disembodied squeak from beneath the cart, 'Aye we're flittin'. The hobgoblin was never going to let him alone.

string of grouse butts where the way gently curves left and shortly meets a wide crossing track. Turn right and follow it along the broad spine of Rudland Rigg. Before covering ½ mile (800m), you will reach a prominent crossroads **B**, where you should turn sharp right.

The way leads back across the head of West Gill before beginning a gradual descent into Farndale. Farther on, as the gradient becomes more purposeful, ignore a track off right, and soon leave the moor, dropping through a gate to continue down a rough field. Finally reaching a lane at the bottom, opposite Monket House, turn right and walk down to a junction **C**.

*If you want to call at the Feversham Arms at Church Houses, you will have to make a small detour, following the lane left into the bottom of the valley. To rejoin the main route at **D**, take a track, signed to*

Low Mill, which you will find on the right, immediately in front of the pub.

? What is the penalty for plucking or injuring Farndale's daffodils?

Otherwise, keep ahead at the junction and continue down the road. After 200 yds (183m), just before a wooden bench, go over a stile on the left, signed 'Church Houses'. Walk down, crossing a stile to reach a bridge over the River Dove, hidden in the trees at the bottom. In a small pasture on the other side, bear right, leaving over a stile onto a

The walk ends along Farndale

track near the café at High Mill **D**.

Follow the track between the cottages, passing through a gate into a small meadow beyond. A flagged path leads from one field to the next. At the far end of the third enclosure, pass through the lower of two gates in the boundary. Twisting and weaving, the river snakes its way down the valley, and while the path does not always follow its bank, the surfaced way is clear. One mile (1.6km) of easy walking ultimately leads you over a bridge and back to the car park. ∎

From Rudland Rigg to Farndale

Further Information

Walking Safety

Although the reasonably gentle countryside that is the subject of this book offers no real dangers to walkers at any time of the year, it is still advisable to take sensible precautions and follow certain well-tried guidelines.

Danby Lodge Moors Centre

Always take with you both warm and waterproof clothing and sufficient food and drink. Wear suitable footwear such as strong walking boots or shoes that give a good grip over stony ground, on slippery slopes and in muddy conditions. Try to obtain a local weather forecast and bear it in mind before you start. Do not be

Repairing stone walls requires an expert hand

afraid to abandon your proposed route and return to your starting point in the event of a sudden and unexpected deterioration in the weather.

All the walks described in this book will be safe to do, given due care and respect, even during the winter. Indeed, a crisp, fine winter day often provides perfect walking conditions, with firm ground underfoot and a clarity unique to this time of the year.

The most difficult hazard likely to be encountered is mud, especially when walking along woodland and field paths, farm tracks and bridleways – the latter in particular can often get churned up by cyclists and horses. In summer, an additional difficulty may be narrow and overgrown paths, particularly along the edges of cultivated fields. Neither should constitute a major problem provided that the appropriate footwear is worn.

Global Positioning System (GPS)
What is GPS?
Global Positioning System, or GPS for short, is a fully-functional navigation system that uses a network of satellites to calculate positions, which are then transmitted to hand-held receivers. By measuring the time it takes a signal to reach the receiver, the distance from the satellite can be estimated. Repeat this with several satellites and the receiver can then triangulate its position, in effect telling the receiver exactly where you are, in any weather, day or night, anywhere on Earth.

GPS information, in the form of grid reference data, is increasingly being used in Pathfinder® guidebooks, and many readers find the

Helmsley is an attractive market town

positional accuracy GPS affords a reassurance, although its greatest benefit comes when you are walking in remote, open countryside or through forests.

GPS has become a vital global utility, indispensable for modern navigation on land, sea and air around the world, as well as an important tool for map-making and land surveying.

Across the fields to Helmsley Castle

Follow the Country Code

- Be safe – plan ahead and follow any signs
- Leave gates and property as you find them
- Protect plants and animals, and take your litter home
- Keep dogs under close control
- Consider other people

(Natural England)

Useful Organisations

Campaign to Protect Rural England
CPRE National Office,
128 Southwark Street, London
SE1 0SW
Tel. 020 7981 2800
www.cpre.org.uk

Camping and Caravanning Club
Greenfields House, Westwood
Way, Coventry CV4 8JH
Site bookings Tel. 0845 130 7633
www.campingandcaravanningclub.co.uk

Campaign for National Parks
6-7 Barnard Mews, London
SW11 1QU
Tel. 020 7924 4077
www.cnp.org.uk

English Heritage
Customer Services Department,
PO Box 569, Swindon SN2 2YP
Tel. 0870 333 1181
www.english-heritage.org.uk
Regional Office
Tel. 01904 601901

Forestry Commission
North York Moors Forest District
Outgang Road, Pickering,
North Yorkshire

YO18 7EL
Tel. 01751 472771
www.forestry.gov.uk

Forest Holidays
Bath Yard, Moira, Derbyshire
DE12 6BA
Tel. 0845 130 8224
www.forestholidays.co.uk

National Trust
Membership and general enquiries
PO Box 39, Warrington
WA5 7WD
Tel. 0844 800 1895
www.nationaltrust.org.uk
Regional Office
Goddards, 27 Tadcaster Road,
Dringhouses, York
YO24 1GG
Tel. 01904 702021

Natural England
1 East Parade, Sheffield
S1 2ET
Tel. 0114 241 8920
www.naturalengland.org.uk

North York Moors National Park
The Old Vicarage, Bondgate,
Helmsley YO62 5BP
Tel. 01439 770657
www.northyorkmoors.org.uk

Visitor Centres

Sutton Bank National Park Visitor Centre, Sutton Bank, Thirsk YO7 2EH
Private Tel. 01845 597426
The Moors Centre, Danby, Whitby YO21 2NB
Private Tel. 01439 772737

North Yorkshire Moors Railway
Pickering Station
Tel. 01751 472508
www.nymr.co.uk

Ordnance Survey
Romsey Road, Maybush, Southampton SO16 4GU
Tel. 08456 05 05 05 (Lo-call)
www.ordnancesurvey.co.uk

Public Transport
Traveline – Tel. 0871 200 22 33
www.traveline.org.uk
Moorsbus – Tel. 01845 597000
www.visitnorthyorkshiremoors.co.uk

Ramblers' Association
2nd Floor, Camelford House, 87-90 Albert Embankment, London SE1 7TW
Tel. 020 7339 8500
www.ramblers.org.uk

Tourist Information
Yorkshire Tourist Board
312 Tadcaster Road, York YO24 1GS
www.yorkshire.com

Local Tourist Information Centres
Great Ayton
Tel. 01642 722835
Guisborough
Tel. 01287 633801
Helmsley
Tel. 01439 770173
Low Dalby
Tel. 01751 460295
Normanby
Tel. 01642 459629
Pickering
Tel. 01751 473791
Pinchinthorpe
Tel. 01287 631132
Ravenscar
Tel. 01723 870138/870423
Saltburn
Tel. 01287 622422
Scarborough
Tel. 01723 383636
Thirsk
Tel. 01845 522755
Whitby
Tel. 01723 383637

Yorkshire Wildlife Trust
1 St George's Place, York,
YO24 1GN
Tel. 01904 659570
www.ywt.org.uk

Youth Hostels Association
Trevelyan House, Dimple Road,
Matlock. Derbyshire DE4 3YH
Tel. 01629 592700
www.yha.org.uk

Ordnance Survey maps of North York Moors

Explorer maps: OL26 (North York Moors – Western area)
OL27 (North York Moors – Eastern area)

Answers to Questions

Walk 1: The sandy path gives you a clue – sandstone.

Walk 2: 1857 – you will find the date on a stone plaque by the bottom of the steps at the start of the walk. In fact the coating of limewash was finally completed on 4 November.

Walk 3: They assisted ladies and the less nimble in remounting their horses after attending a church service.

Walk 4: Look above its doorway for the date – 1790.

Walk 5: The symbols for 11 of Britain's National Parks. Can you find the one for this park, Young Ralph's Cross?

Walk 6: The crow, a large, black bird, not dissimilar to a rook. It is sometimes said that if you see a rook on its own, it is probably a crow, but a flock of crows are more likely to be rooks.

Walk 7: An acorn, depicted in the monument at the end of the walk and used to mark each of the country's 15 National Trails.

Walk 8: A fox. The stone is actually a gravemarker, carved for Bobbie Dowson, who served as whip to the hounds of the Bilsdale Hunt.

Walk 9: Crayfish – check the information panel by the car park to discover what else to look out for.

Walk 10: An ancient stone coffin, shaped to hold the corpse.

Walk 11: An inscription on the monument relates that he was killed at Owhyhee on February 14, 1799.

Walk 12: On the west screen and lectern, they are the trademark of the Robert Thompson workshop at Kilburn.

Walk 13: St Peter, he is the patron saint of fishermen.

Walk 14: An information panel explains how coastguards trained here, firing rescue rockets at a post erected to simulate a ship's mast.

Walk 15: A well to St Cedd is on the right as you walk to the church and another to St Chad lies on the right as you climb out of the village towards the moor.

Walk 16: 13th-century tiles, decorated with geometric patterns in yellow and green. Some survive in the abbey and more are displayed in the small museum there.

Walk 17: A nearby stone tablet indicates it was probably dug by 13th-century monks from Malton Priory, as a watering hole for their grazing livestock.

Walk 18: Look on the gate – the 'Penalty for Neglect' is £2.

Walk 19: Read the information board at the Alum Works to discover it was a canon, which you can see in the National Trust Coastal Centre at the end of the walk.

Walk 20: A notice by the car park tells you it is £5. Of course, you should not pick any wild flowers, but leave them for others to enjoy and allow them to re-seed for the following year.

Crimson Walking Guides

Crimson Short Walks

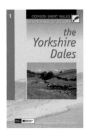

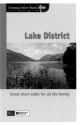

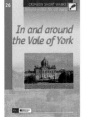

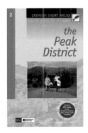

Pathfinder® Guides

North York Moors — Walks

Durham, North Pennines and Tyne & Wear — WALKS

Yorkshire Dales — WALKS

Vale of York and the Yorkshire Wolds — Walks

Lake District Central Lakeland — Walks

Lake District Eastern Lakeland — Walks

Lake District North & West Lakeland — Walks

Lake District West & South Lakeland — Walks

For more information visit www.totalwalking.co.uk
Sales: 020 8334 1730
email: info@portfoliobooks.com

crimsonPUBLISHING

Unearth...

Easy to navigate... informative and packed with practical information

Which? Holiday

The best of Britain series

ACCESSIBLE, CONTEMPORARY GUIDES BY LOCAL EXPERTS

Cornwall and the Isles of Scilly
ISBN: 978 1 85458 424 3

Cotswolds
ISBN: 978 1 85458 463 2

Devon
ISBN: 978 1 85458 426 7

East Anglia
ISBN: 978 1 85458 423 6

Isle of Wight and the New Forest
ISBN: 978 1 85458 422 9

The Lake District
ISBN: 978 1 85458 425 0

COMING SOON...

Edinburgh: 978 1 85458 464 9
Northern Ireland: 978 1 85458 465 6
The Peak District: 978 1 85458 467 0

Buy your guide at **www.crimsonpublishing.co.uk**